Eating Ramen

A Survival Guide for Tough Financial Times

by Ellie Byrd

Leigh Walker Books

Published by arrangement with
Leigh Walker Books
Atlanta, Georgia

10 9 8 7 6 5 4 3 2 1

ISBN 978-1-930521-10-0

Forward by Lew Forbes

Told in an extraordinarily touching, personal and revealing manner, this book has the capacity to change your life. Although many of these powerful concepts are wrapped around financial terms, the reality is that they apply far beyond the financial arena.

OK, let's be honest. This book is not for everyone. This is a book for people who can handle straight forward advice and are willing to take the steps, sometimes austere, to live up to their values and desires. If you are one of those people, please keep reading. You have absolutely come to the right place!

As Ellie explains, we can overcome setbacks, some repeatedly and some that are personally devastating, and despite them, (or maybe because of them) we can actually achieve far more than we ever dreamed possible. As we are going through these challenging periods, the road may be difficult, frightening and overwhelming at times. But in the end, if this is something we truly believe and desire, we may well resurrect ourselves and create some of the most precious and priceless memories of our entire lives. The process requires determination and commitment. It's a process that enables us to learn good things about ourselves and grow into a new and better person. Once we have faced and conquered our challenges, we will never be the same person again and our vision of everything from that day forward will be different.

This book is a fascinating story, told from the heart, of someone who faced adversity, struggled to overcome it and succeeded beyond belief. This book is also a guide, complete with worksheets and step-by-step instructions, for those who want to embark on their own journey. If any of this sounds interesting to you, please keep reading and you will be richly rewarded. You don't have to agree with everything in this book or follow every possible recommendation. That's okay. Just use what makes sense in your life and prepare to enjoy the benefits.

Good luck to you!

Lew Forbes
CFP®, CRPC®, MBA

Dedication

This book was a labor of love that was over three years in the making. Many thanks to my friends and family for putting up with me while I wrote it. There were countless late nights and many things I should have done that I didn't while I sat in front of the computer screen. Sheila, thanks for the hours you spent talking with me about the tiniest details to be sure I got the point across correctly. Bill, thanks for your encouragement and suggestions. David, thank you for reading it and deciding that I needed so much help that you linked me to two more editors! Nancy, your love and support is unconditional. You always believe in me, so much so that I have to believe in myself! And to my Entrepreneurs' Organization Forum, thanks for the endless words of encouragement and for holding me accountable to getting it done. You guys rock!

– *Ellie Byrd*

Preface

I've been broke three times in my life. Each time, the cause was completely different and completely unexpected. And each time I dug my way back out of the hole – slowly, carefully and sometimes painfully. I leaned on a combination of lessons learned from my frugal upbringing, my will to survive and a passion for common sense. While being broke isn't something to be proud of, it does give me the courage to consider myself something of an expert at surviving tough financial times. I did it three times. I could do it again if I had to. I hope I don't.

This book is organized in five sections, one for each time I was broke, one for my method of financial recovery (the Ramen Method) and the last for some great and economical recipes.

- **Section 1: Stop the Bleeding.**
  This was my most recent financial debacle, in 2002. As a small business owner, my business was struggling through the economic downturn in 2001, and by 2002, I was nearly bankrupt. This was probably the scariest of my three situations. In this section, I talk about what I did personally to cut back to the bare minimum.

- **Section 2: Living Broke... The First Time**
  This was the first time I had nothing. After an unexpected turn of events, I had to drop out of college and get a job to support myself. These were some of the leanest times of my life, but they equipped me with unwavering determination. I've been able to draw on that strength many times since.

- **Section 3: Till Divorce Do Us Part**
  My second experience with being broke happened after my marriage fell apart. Interestingly, money was part of the problem. We had money, we just couldn't agree on how to spend it or save it. Before long, I was out on my own again, calling on my old survival tactics to weather the storm.

- **Section 4: The Ramen Method**
  After living through three bouts of financial devastation, I developed what I call "The Ramen Method". It's a simple, three-step process to help people get on the right track financially. With the help of some basic diagrams and a ramen noodle, I'll illustrate the path to financial independence – or financial ruin depending on how you manage your money. As a bonus, the process can be applied to other non-financial challenges.

- **Section 5: Ramen Noodle Recipes**
  How can you beat dinner for 17 cents? Ramen noodles are a great way to have a cheap meal. They've been a staple in my diet for years, not just because they're cheap, but because I like them! I thought I was the only nut case who was inventing low cost meals by doctoring up my ramen noodles. I was pleasantly surprised to find that lots of people have been inventing ramen noodle recipes for years. So I've included a selection of recipes for your cooking and dining pleasure. It seemed like the right way to end the book!

Throughout the book, I have included exercises and tools for the reader to use when working on their own financial recovery. You can download the worksheets free at www.eatingramen.com. Even if you're not broke, some of these tools may be helpful to you in managing your own financial situation. At the same time, I hope you might gain a new perspective on debt, wealth and even happiness.

Table of Contents

Chapter 1: Stop The Bleeding

Chapter 2: Living Broke... The First Time

Chapter 3: Till Divorce Do Us Part

Chapter 4: The Ramen Method

Chapter 5: Ramen Noodle Recipes

1

Stop The Bleeding

*"I have not failed.
I've just found 10,000 ways
that won't work."*

Thomas Edison, American inventor and businessman;
founder of General Electric; holder of 1,093 patents;
inventions include the phonograph and the light bulb

2   Eating Ramen

Inc. 500 to Shrink 500

My company was already in trouble after Y2K. All the technology projects came screeching to a halt because everyone had finished preparing for the new millennium. *Happy New Year! Happy New Century! Now, let's table all of our technology projects for the next few years. After all, haven't we spent enough money on technology lately?* It was the beginning of a new century and the beginning of lean times for companies like mine that serviced the technology industry.

And then came the tragedy of 9/11. At our prime, we had 30 employees and a stable of contractors. Now, most of them were sitting on the bench, and I had no work coming in. How was I going to make payroll? As the founder and sole owner of the company, the responsibility was all mine. At first, I thought we could weather the storm. I did all the right things – I contacted loyal customers, offered discounted rates, updated our website and marketing materials, started praying with a passion. But nothing worked. No revenues. Ongoing expenses. It was a house of cards, and it couldn't stand for very long.

I was making a lot of mistakes, too, which I can see now in hindsight. The biggest and most devastating mistake to me personally was that I kept people on the payroll far too long – six months too long. In almost 20 years in business, I had never laid anyone off, and for a while, I thought we could make it through and I could keep my perfect record. We'd been through tough time before. In years past, I had secretly taken myself off the payroll, for weeks or months at a time, in order to make sure my employees got paid and felt secure with their job. But I had already stopped paying myself over a year ago. Now what?

So I expanded our line of credit and I ran it up to the max. Then I took out a second mortgage on my house. Next I borrowed against my 401K. Then I got a line of credit on my house. For six months, it enabled me to make payroll. But I'll never forget the day when I hit the wall.

It was March 5, 2002, and I had an appointment with MCI WorldCom to get a signature on a $280,000 project. If we got it, it could hold us for several months. If we didn't, I would have to go back to the office and lay off 90% of my employees.

So let me set the stage. My meeting was with Fred (name changed to protect the guilty), a VP in WorldCom's software development division. He was the guy who would sign the contract, but there was a catch. I wanted--no I *needed* to include a clause on payment. WorldCom had always been terrible about paying us. We used to joke that they must send their employees to a training class to teach them how to delay payment. They had 1,001 excuses.

Sometimes we would wait for six months to get paid. Sometimes we had to hold back our deliverables to force payment. For a huge company like WorldCom that was supposedly riding high, it seemed ridiculous. In actuality, as we were soon to learn, it was a sign of the impending collapse they were about to face.

I had never met Fred before, but he was ready to sign the contract so it didn't matter. It was Phase 2 of a three-phase project, and we had already completed Phase 1 with great accolades from everyone who mattered. We were a shoo-in for the work. If anybody did the job, we would do it. But Fred didn't know about the clause, and I was going to have to talk him into it. It was non-negotiable. I couldn't risk doing the work if we weren't going to get paid. And with WorldCom's payment history, the odds weren't good unless we were paid up front.

Five minutes into the meeting, after I had introduced the clause, I remember Fred yelling at me "Who do you think you are?" along with a string of insults. As he proceeded to kick me out of his plush corner office, his voice escalated to a high, nervous pitch as he screamed, "You'll never do business with WorldCom again!" He was right. The entire meeting lasted less than ten minutes. WorldCom didn't want to commit to paying their own bills, and my employees' lives were in the balance. Their livelihoods were at stake, and one incredibly rude, wildly screaming VP had just sealed their fate.

So that was it. I had to go back to the office and lay off most of my employees. It was one of the hardest things I have ever done. These people had depended on me to provide them with a secure job and an income. It was a huge responsibility and I had managed to do it for nearly 20 years, but now it was over. The company was falling apart and I couldn't help them anymore. I couldn't even afford to give them a severance package. During the layoff process, I learned an important lesson: When you lay people off, they're going to be mad at you. It doesn't matter why you laid them off. It doesn't matter that you second-mortgaged your house. It doesn't matter that they've been making more money than you for the past two years, or that you've been working without a paycheck for so long you've wiped out your savings. I thought we were a family. I thought we had a special relationship. I thought we were all loyal to each other. I thought we were all in this together. But at the end of the day,

> *When you lay people off, it doesn't matter why. They're going to be mad at you.*

we weren't. None of it mattered. They just got laid off and they were mad. Worse yet, I couldn't really blame them.

Lesson learned: I should have laid them off six months

earlier. They could have been mad at me six months sooner, and I could have avoided going half a million dollars into debt.

I had been in business for 19 years, starting out as a contract trainer and creating a company, more by accident than by design. During the early 1990s, we skyrocketed from $100K in revenues up into the millions. At that point, we became a serious contender for the prestigious Inc. 500 list – the list of the 500 fastest-growing companies in the country. But now I wondered if they had an opposite list for companies that were shrinking at equally alarming rates. Why not call it the Shrink 500? At that moment, I could see myself at the top of the list.

I felt like a complete failure.

One Shovel at a Time

Shortly after my debt had soared over $500,000, I was driving through downtown Atlanta when I saw a homeless man on the street holding a sign: *WILL WORK FOR FOOD*. I remember thinking, "He's better off than I am. He may have nothing, but I have *worse* than nothing. I'm drowning in a sea of debt! I owe a lot of people a lot of money—and he doesn't." I didn't just have to start over. I had to dig out of a hole—a **big** hole. It was overwhelming and depressing.

How had I let it get this bad? How was I ever going to recover? I had no idea. All I had ever wanted was to be financially independent, but now the term "financial independence" seemed laughable. The homeless guy had it right. He was financially independent.

> In my heart, bankruptcy was just plain wrong, the easy way out. The big "Oh well."

He didn't owe anybody anything! *I* was the financial disaster.

I contemplated bankruptcy for a short time. It would get the creditors off my back and I could start with a clean slate. Like the homeless guy. The thought was mildly appealing.

But something deep down inside wouldn't let me seriously consider it. In my heart, bankruptcy was just plain wrong, the easy way out. The big "Oh well." There has to be a ripple effect when someone claims bankruptcy, doesn't there? What are we doing to the next guy? If I'm not paying my bills, how is the next guy going to pay his? Aren't we all connected?

Even more importantly, if I filed bankruptcy, what was I saying about my own commitments? To me, bankruptcy is like lying. It's like saying – *"I'm going to pay you. I even signed a contract saying I'm going to pay you. But now I'm not going to pay you. I lied about that. Sorry. And it's okay because there's this legal loophole I can use to get out of paying you. It's called bankruptcy. Good for me. Bad for you. Oh well."*

If I filed bankruptcy, how could anyone ever trust me again? How could I trust myself? Larry Burkett, a Christian author, wrote in *Business By The Book* that even if you claim bankruptcy, you still owe the money. As soon as you're able, you should pay your creditors back even though the law says you don't have to. It's the only way to maintain your integrity. The bankruptcy is just a mechanism for legally keeping the creditors from hounding you while you're digging out of the hole.

In the midst of all this, I sat down for a beer with my friend and mentor, Richard. Richard is a kind, quirky soul – a man who loves guns, music, cats and his wife. He is one of the most intelligent people I know, and he has the ability to see through the clutter and hone in on what's really important. Richard listened to my latest update and pondered for a few moments before declaring, "You've got to stop the bleeding."

I didn't know exactly how I was going to do that, and in Richard's usual style, he wouldn't tell me. He never got tactical with me – he would just make these brilliant statements and leave it to me to figure out the details on my own. Richard was a strategy guy, and he gave me the right strategy: *Stop the bleeding*. I knew his words were spot-on.

I didn't have a wealthy relative to bail me out and my odds of winning the lottery weren't good. I couldn't think of any shortcuts. So I would have to dig my way out, one shovel at a time. I proceeded to embark on a systematic, common-sense approach to stop the bleeding. And that's what the rest of this book is about.

Cut It Off

One of the first things I did was cut off everything that cost money that I didn't absolutely have to have. I was amazed at all the conveniences I had built into my life. There's an old saying: *Time is Money*. Over the years, I had used that saying to justify all kinds of things—the housekeeper, the gardener, the handyman, the mechanic. I figured they were saving me time that I could be using to do more productive and profitable things. And as long as I was employed, that logic worked well. But times had changed. I wasn't earning anything at the moment, so I couldn't keep spending.

If the old saying was *Time is Money*, my new saying was *Money is Oxygen*. Every penny had to count. Everything but food and shelter became a luxury, and with all the bleeding, I couldn't afford luxuries.

So I sat down with my checkbook and I made a list of absolutely everything I was spending money on. Then I started working my way down the list and making cuts. It was embarrassing at first—calling people and telling them I could no longer afford their services. I stumbled around the explanation. *Times are tough. My business is in trouble. I just got laid off.* It didn't much matter which explanation I used; the end result was the same. I couldn't pay them any longer so they had to stop doing whatever it was they had been doing for me. I believed in my heart that I would someday be making the reverse call, asking these people to restart my service. And I told them that. But for now, I simply couldn't pay.

Most people were incredibly kind when I called to discontinue service. One woman offered to pray for me, and I cried when I hung up the phone. A few people tried to sell me a cheaper version or offer payment terms, but I had to hold firm. No more money going out. *Period!* Only one guy was rude and I immediately made a note to myself: *Never use this guy again!*

So here was my list:

- **Paper service.** I could get the news from the TV or the internet or my friends.

- **Yard service.** I borrowed the neighbor's lawn mower and got some exercise.

- **Yard chemicals.** My green grass turned brown within a few months after the chemical company stopped sprinkling their magic dust on my yard. But I noticed that other yards in my neighborhood were suffering a similar fate. Perhaps I was not alone in my plight!

- **Cleaning lady.** Ouch. Over the years, my cleaning lady had become a friend and I was going to miss her friendship as much as her cleaning.

- **Magazine subscriptions.** This one was easy. I just didn't renew them when the bills came in.

- **Security alarm service.** The alarm still worked (loud sirens during a break-in); it just wasn't connected to the central alarm company. I left the alarm company's signs prominently displayed in the

> I still left the signs in the windows and the yard, saying that I had an alarm service. How would the burglars know it wasn't connected?

windows and the yard. How would burglars know the alarm wasn't connected to anything?

- **Long distance phone service.** I found I could drop the phone company's long-distance service and buy a pre-paid calling card. The rates were significantly lower.

- **Exterminator.** My bug man used to come out twice a year for about $80 a pop. After I cut him off, I've never called him back because I learned that I never needed him in the first place!

- **Cable TV.** Now this one was REALLY hard. But I reminded myself that my parents once survived on no TV at all, much less cable TV. I could do it too. And I vowed to use the time savings on making money to dig me out of the hole.

- **Health club.** Yes, I would have to pay an initiation fee when I rejoined, but that wasn't a reason to keep spending money now. (And in an ironic twist of fate, when I finally renewed several years later, the health club waived the fee.)

- **Car wash.** I used to drive up, hand someone my keys, sit down in the air-conditioning and watch my clean car come out the other end of a long tunnel, all shiny and white again. No more. A bucket, a garden hose and some soap were all I needed.

Of course, everyone's list of cutbacks will be different. Monthly memberships, annual memberships, automatic credit card charges, Weight Watchers meetings, movie club, etc. The important thing is to make the list and make the cutbacks. I freed up over $450 a month with one day of phone calls.

Worksheet: Cut Off List – Sample

For anyone who is inclined to go on this financial journey with me, I've included worksheets throughout this book that illustrate the steps I followed. Use them or skip them as you prefer. It's my hope that if any of you are struggling right now financially, these worksheets and tools might give you a roadmap to help you dig your way out of debt and get back on your feet.

This worksheet focuses on eliminating expenses that you don't absolutely have to have. One call can end most of these payments, but be careful about vendors who may assess a penalty if you discontinue service early. Always ask, "Is there a penalty for discontinuing this service?".

✓ Done	Things I cut-off, stopped or cancelled	Estimated Monthly Savings
✓	Newspaper service	$22
✓	Magazines	$12
✓	Yard service, yard chemicals	$125
✓	House cleaning service	$100
✓	Security alarm	$22
✓	Cable TV	$34
✓	Long distance phone	$7
✓	Exterminator	$15
✓	Annual heating and A/C maintenance	$31
✓	Health club	$49
✓	Diet club (Weight Watchers, Nutrisystem, etc.)	$18
✓	Car wash	$19

My total estimated monthly savings: $ 454.00   .

Worksheet: Cut Off List – Try It!

Stop paying for things that aren't a necessity for survival.

1) Check items off the list as you stop or cancel them. Estimate how much money you will save each month and write it in the right-hand column. Skip items that don't apply to you.

2) Next, add items to the list to make it your own. Include anything you pay for or that is automatically billed to you on a weekly, monthly or other regular basis that is not necessary for survival. Write them in the blank lines and estimate the monthly savings for each one.

3) Add up the estimated amounts to see your total estimated monthly savings!

✓ Done	Things to cut-off, stop or cancel	Estimated Monthly Savings
	Newspaper service	
	Magazines	
	Yard service, yard chemicals	
	House cleaning service	
	Security alarm	
	Cable TV	
	Long distance phone	
	Exterminator	
	Annual heating and A/C maintenance	
	Health club	
	Diet club (Weight Watchers, Nutrisystem, etc.)	
	Car wash	

My total estimated monthly savings: $_____

Download this worksheet free at www.eatingramen.com.

Cut It Back

There were some things I couldn't eliminate entirely, but I could still cut back on them. Take insurance, for example. I had to keep my car insurance, but could I cut back the charges? I called State Farm and explained my dilemma. I said I wanted to shave $100 off my annual charge, and my agent worked it out with a combination of decreased coverage and increased deductible. Done.

I did the same thing with homeowner's insurance—decreased the coverage and increased the deductible. Done.

Same thing with health insurance. Increase the deductible and reduce the payment. It amazed me how helpful the insurance companies were. They really worked with me, and, thankfully, they didn't make me feel bad about the cut-backs. I think they were happy to keep my business—at any level.

Next, I headed to the bank. I was holding several loans now: my home's primary mortgage, the second mortgage and the line of credit. Could I consolidate them all under one loan and reduce the monthly payment?

When I met with my banker, I realized the importance of communication. My banker told me that lots of people who are in financial distress just bury their head in the sand and try to ignore what's happening. They start paying their bills late or stop paying them altogether. They never call to talk about it or explain what's going on. They never ask for help. "If people would just come in and talk with us," he explained, "we'd put our heads together and try to figure out a way to make this work for them. We aren't the bad guys. We don't want them to default."

Bottom line: my bank worked with me and we structured a better arrangement.

> "If people would just come in and talk with us," my banker explained, "we'd put our heads together and try to figure out a way to make this work. We aren't the bad guys. We don't want them to default."

I promised to come in every month and let them know how things were going. If I was going to miss a payment, they would know about it in advance. And they would know what I was doing to try to fix it. They wouldn't have to chase me down—I would be first in line to keep them informed.

There were other things I did to cut back, too. I used to have my teeth cleaned twice a year and I cut back to once a year. I waited longer to change the oil in my car. I ran around the house and unplugged any unused electrical appliances to keep them from draining energy. These were small things, but over time, they all added up.

I don't know how much money men spend on their hair, but I was paying close to $100 a month at a nice salon for a cut and style. Every 90 days, I paid an additional $200 for hair color and highlights. No more. I started getting my hair cut for $10 at Great Clips or Walmart, and I learned how to put highlights in my own hair using a $12 box from Walgreens. My sister was great at helping me, but I even learned to do it on my own.

I was determined not to turn on the heat or the A/C in my house until my finances were back on track. The pioneers survived without heating or air conditioning. Why couldn't I? If anyone had dropped in unexpectedly during the winter, they would have found me walking around the house with double socks and slippers and as many layers as I could wear and still move. I would sleep upstairs (because hot air rises) under a huge pile of blankets and quilts. I put socks on my hands like little mittens to keep my fingers warm. When summer arrived, I walked around the house in a swimsuit, hair pulled back, living downstairs (because hot air rises). I kept a spray bottle with me at all times to spray myself down, and I could step in front of the fan to feel momentarily cooler. I slept on an air mattress with an oscillating fan blowing in my face. In an occasional moment of decadence, I would stick my head in the freezer, but the guilt would never let me stay in there for very long.

I was awfully glad that I didn't have a car payment during my financial crisis. If I did, I would have sold the car and bought whatever car I could get with the cash, no matter how old and beaten it was. And if I hadn't needed the car to meet with customers, I would have shifted to a bicycle or public transportation. If I was going to stop the bleeding, I couldn't live beyond my means.

Another change I made was to go through the mail only once a week. Most of it was bad news anyway, and why bring myself down every day by looking at the unpaid bills. I threw all the mail into a basket and once a week on Monday night, I went through everything all at once. I could get depressed for an evening and be done with it for the week. An unexpected side benefit was the time savings. I become extremely efficient at going through the mail in bulk, separating the junk from the important stuff and handling what needed to be handled in a single sweep.

With all the cutbacks, I had shaved another $394 off my monthly expenses. It felt good to be proactively doing something. I could hear Richard's voice in my head repeating his advice, *"Stop the bleeding."* Okay, Richard. I'm working on it.

Worksheet: Cut Back List – Sample

This worksheet focuses on reducing expenses that cannot be eliminated. I was amazed at how much money I saved on insurance by increasing the deductible and reducing the coverage – especially in areas where I didn't really need the coverage to begin with. Who knew! If I hadn't asked, I would have continued paying for things I didn't use or need forever.

✓ Done	Things I cut back or reduced	Estimated Monthly Savings
✓	Car Insurance	$17
✓	Renter's / Homeowner's Insurance	$10
✓	Health Insurance	$67
✓	Credit Card Companies (interest rates, consolidation)	n/a
✓	Student loans (interest rates, consolidation)	n/a
✓	Home/Apartment – downsize, lower monthly payment, get a roomate	$200
✓	Car – downsize, lower monthly payment	n/a
✓	Hair Salon, facial, manicure/pedicure, etc.	$100

My total estimated monthly savings: $ 394.00   .

*n/a = not applicable. I was lucky that I didn't have any credit card debt, student loans or a car payment at the time.

Worksheet: Cut Back List – Try It!

Everything is negotiable. How can you reduce the amount of money you are spending? Call vendors and providers and ask them to **work with you** to help lower your bill. Ask them if you can raise the deductible, lower coverage, reduce interest rates or fees, etc.

1) Check items off the list as you make the cut back. Estimate how much money you will save each month and write it in the right-hand column.

2) Next, continue the list by adding everything else you can think of that you buy, consume or pay money for. Think about how you can reduce (or eliminate) the cost. Get creative!

✓ Done	Things to cut back, reduce or temporarily eliminate	Estimated Monthly Savings
	Car Insurance	
	Renter's / Homeowner's Insurance	
	Health Insurance	
	Credit Card Companies (interest rates, consolidation)	
	Student loans (interest rates, consolidation)	
	Home/Apartment – downsize, lower monthly payment	
	Car – downsize, lower monthly payment	
	Hair Salon, facial, manicure/pedicure, etc.	

My total estimated monthly savings: $_____.

Download this worksheet free at www.eatingramen.com.

Downsize the Stuff

George Carlin did a great skit on "stuff". (Check it out on YouTube.) He said we all have loads of stuff, and our houses are just places to store all our stuff, kind of like big boxes with a lid on it. If we didn't have so much stuff in the first place, then we wouldn't need such big houses. Some of us have so much stuff, we have to put some of our stuff into storage. That's why you can't have everything—where would you put it?

I travel frequently with my work and as a consultant, I've had occasion to temporarily live in another city for as long as three months. During these mini-moves, I would take a subset of my stuff and live in very small quarters that were a fraction of the size of my house. And guess what? I survived just fine. In fact, I kind of liked it. Simple. Uncluttered. In fact, I'm on a tear right now to downsize and get rid of a lot more stuff.

Think about it. We come into this world without any stuff. We spend a lot of our lives accumulating stuff. But God knows we can't take any of our stuff with us when we go, so at some point, we have to start getting rid of stuff. After all, why do we need so much stuff?

What really matters? What are we going to do with all that stuff anyway? Can't we clean out the clutter and get rid of some of this stuff?

Here's an interesting exercise: Imagine you had to move into a small 10' x 20' efficiency apartment. What would you take? Having traveled to India, Thailand and Indonesia, I've seen entire families living in smaller spaces. So it's entirely possible. We've just grown up in a society where bigger is better and we're used to living in big houses with lots of stuff. But do we really need it?

And speaking of the house....

For many people, the monthly rent or house payment is the single biggest expense they have every month. That being the case, doesn't it make sense to look at where we're living and how much we're paying? I had to look at my house and consider moving to a smaller space, or

> *We've grown up in a society where bigger is better and we're used to having big houses with lots of stuff.*

at minimum, taking on a roommate. It was the last thing I wanted to do, but I was in survival mode. Need versus want. I didn't really need the big house all to myself, I just wanted it. So I took in a roommate. I missed my privacy but I loved the financial help. It was more than worth it.

And as for all the stuff, a lot of it was really easy to get rid of. Places like the Salvation Army, Goodwill and the Battered Women's Shelter survive on people getting rid of stuff. A great way to get started is to go through the house and gather up anything you haven't used in five years. Arguably, if you haven't used it in five years, odds are you're never going to use it. Of course, there may be a few nostalgic items that you can't bear to part with, and that's okay. It's all the other stuff that can help to un-clutter your life.

In the midst of my crisis, I took three truckloads of "stuff" to the Battered Women's Shelter. It seemed ironic. Here I was, broke and scared; but for some reason it felt really good to give things away. No matter how bad things seemed for me at the moment, there were other people who were in a lot worse shape than me. I remember driving up to the appointed meeting place at a gas station and transferring everything from my van to hers. The lady explained that they wouldn't give out the location of the shelter for security reasons. This was the only safe way to make a donation – meeting in a public place like a gas station. That smacked me in the face like a brick. I may be scared about how I was going to pay the bills, but at least I wasn't in fear for my life.

So I got a double benefit by giving some things away. I simplified my life and cleared out the clutter, plus I got to feel good about helping others at the same time. Now, that's **good** stuff!

Create a Budget

The next step in my plan was to create a budget. Thanks to my lessons from my money-wise parents, I knew there were two parts to a budget: income and expenses. Income is the amount of money coming in and expenses is the amount of money going out.

I had no income to speak of, so I started on the expenses side. From my previous accounting experience, I knew this was kind of like working the budget backwards. Normally, you should start with what you have coming in and then figure out what you can afford to spend in expenses. To quote Thomas Jefferson, "Never spend your money before you have it."

The problem was, I didn't have any money to start with (in fact, I was in debt) and I didn't have any money coming in. So I had to figure out the bare minimum of what my expenses were every month and let that dictate how much money I needed to earn in order to pay the bills. Here's the process I used:

1) I started with the regular monthly expenses – the power bill, the water bill, the mortgage payment, etc. I also had to include things like my car insurance, which only came twice a year, and my homeowner's association fee, which only came once a year. I used a spreadsheet

to do this, although a simple sheet of paper would have worked just fine.

2) Once I finished the list, I divided all my expenses into two categories: fixed expenses and variable expenses. Fixed expenses are the ones that are exactly the same every month, so this would include things like the rent or mortgage payment, car payment, loan payments and health insurance premiums. Then I moved to the variable expenses—utility bills, gas for my car, food, clothes, sundries. The list of variable expenses was significantly longer, but I also noted that it would be easier to reduce those costs with planning and creativity. (More on that later.)

3) Then, I prioritized the list of variable expenses. My thinking was this: I would pay the fixed expenses first, because if I didn't do that, I'd totally screw up my credit rating. After all the fixed expenses were paid, I could start chipping away at the variable expenses in priority order. But at some point, I wouldn't be able to spend any more. If I didn't have enough money to buy clothes, for example, I didn't buy clothes. In fact,

> I used to live in fear that my friends would nominate me for the TV show "What Not To Wear".

clothes were such a low priority that I actually went for

two and a half years without buying any new clothes, not even a pair of socks. I used to live in fear that my friends would nominate me for the TV show "What Not To Wear." They were seeing the same old clothes on me over and over. The clothes were looking worn and the styles were terribly outdated. When I did finally start buying clothes again, I started at the thrift shop. There was a wonderful thrift store that had an annual sale where you could take a brown paper grocery bag and fill it up with as many clothes as you could shove into that bag for a cost of just $5. It was fantastic! I bought shoes, coats, dresses, shorts, shirts, pants, etc. I remember getting a London Fog coat that I still have to this day. The style is timeless, and when I found it, it looked like it had never been worn. With all the other clothes I stuffed in that bag, I figure that coat cost me about 25 cents. It must have been worth over $100. What a deal!

4) I projected my expenses three years in advance. Then I started plugging numbers into the *Income* column. *How much did I have to make each month in order to make ends meet.* No matter what the number was, it seemed high and I had no earthly idea how I was going to get the money. But at least I had a target.

I didn't dare dream of getting ahead yet; I just wanted to stop sliding further into debt. At the end of the day, I needed to bring in $2,427 per month in income. So that was it. That was my target. Now it was time to roll up my sleeves and get to work.

Worksheet: Create Your Budget – Sample

My budget was pitiful – no income, all expenses. Even so, my one-sided budget showed me how much I needed to earn in order to pay my expenses. These are my "survival" expenses only.

Description	Amount	Subtotal
Income		
+Wages	.00	
+Unemployment	.00	
+Alimony/Child Support	.00	
+Investment Income	.00	
+Other Income	.00	.00
Expenses		
-Rent or Mortgage	1400.00	
-Home Equity Loans	330.00	
-Auto Insurance (paid semi-annually)	103.00	
-Homeowner's Insurance (paid annually)	45.00	
-Homeowner's Association fees (paid annually)	31.00	
-Health Insurance	217.00	
-Utilities: Electric	45.00	
-Utilities: Gas	35.00	
-Utilities: Water	21.00	
-Utilities: Trash	52.00	
-Telephone	24.00	
-Gas, Filter & Oil	44.00	
-Food	80.00	2,427.00

My Projected Earnings (or Loss) per Month: $___- 2,247 (loss)___.

Worksheet: Create Your Budget – Try It!

Creating a budget is easier than it looks. Just follow these easy steps.
1) List every source of income and how much you earn on average each month. Add more lines if needed.
2) List every "survival" expense and how much you spend on average each month. Add more lines if needed.
3) Subtotal each category, then subtract Expenses from Income. Voila! You have a budget.

Description	Amount	Subtotal
Income		
+Wages		
+Unemployment		
+Alimony/Child Support		
+Investment Income		
+Part-time Job		
+Other Income		
Expenses		
-Rent or Mortgage		
-Home Equity Loans		
-Car Loan Payment		
-Auto Insurance (paid semi-annually)		
-Homeowner's Insurance (paid annually)		
-Alimony/Child Support		
-Child Care		
-Health Insurance		
-Utilities: Electric		
-Utilities: Gas		
-Utilities: Water		
-Utilities: Trash		
-Credit Card Payoff Amount		
-Telephone		
-Gas, Filter & Oil		
-Food		

My Projected Earnings (or Loss) per Month: $_____.

Download this worksheet free at www.eatingramen.com.

Roll Up Your Sleeves and Get to Work

So far I had trimmed a lot of fat, but it still wasn't enough. To get through this mess and dig my way out of debt, I needed to roll up my sleeves. I was still in a negative cash flow situation and I needed to change that.

I decided I could save money by doing things myself. For the first time in my life, I put transmission fluid in my car. I felt like I was in a foreign country when I walked into the auto parts store, but thankfully, the guy behind the counter took pity on me and helped me out. He talked me through everything and showed me exactly what I needed to do, step by step. It felt so good

> *I felt like I was in a foreign country when I walked into the auto parts store to buy transmission fluid.*

to successfully do something under the hood of my car, I went back to the store and bought some windshield-wiper fluid and filled that up myself. Next came a book on how to change the oil. After browsing the book, I decided an oil change was beyond my skills and I'd probably cause more damage than I could ever save. Thankfully, a friend helped me out so I didn't have to do it myself. But I had the bug. I even learned how to put air in my tires.

From that moment on, before I spent any money on anything I asked myself if it was possible for me to do it myself. Changing the air filters on the furnace, fixing a broken chair, repairing the mailbox. It was amazing how many times the answer was "Yes, I can do that!" New horizons.

Next I needed to come up with ways to make money. In an unfortunate twist of fate, I couldn't even collect unemployment because I hadn't been drawing a paycheck for so long. Technically, I was no longer an employee, so there was no way to collect.

So I needed to earn money the old-fashioned way – with a job. My first real job at age 14 was flipping burgers and I knew I could get a job doing that, but they only paid minimum wage and I needed to earn more than minimum wage. I needed to earn $2,427 per month to be exact. According to my calculations, it would take me 560 hours at minimum wage to earn enough money to pay my monthly expenses. There just weren't enough hours in a month so it was physically impossible. Maybe if I had kids, they could get jobs flipping burgers and together we could make ends meet. But I didn't have any kids so it was all on my shoulders.

I started with a garage sale and pulled in over $500 in one weekend. But I couldn't keep doing that every weekend or my house would be empty in no time!

So I looked for project work, something I was

intimately familiar with from the old days. Project work meant writing curriculum and teaching classes for corporate clients. I hadn't worked on a project myself in years. I had morphed into the lead salesperson at my company. But now it was time for me to put myself back into billable work. I took in projects at 50% of what I normally would have charged through my company. But I desperately needed the work and it was income. It was a good start. I took on as many projects and side jobs as I could physically work, and I braced myself for 7-day workweeks and 12-hour days. I took on piece-meal work, odd jobs, anything that would bring in money. I even reverted back to an old talent—playing the piano—and I started moonlighting in bars and restaurants on the weekend. The tip jar was my salary and I treasured every dollar in that jar.

It all added up. It took me almost six months to get there, but I finally reached the point where I was steadily pulling in over two thousand dollars per month, and the amount kept climbing. I was getting back in the saddle. I started paying off my debt, but I was nowhere near ready to celebrate. It was going to take a **long** time to earn back half a million dollars.

Thankfully, I never had to flip burgers, but I would have if it came to that. I'm not above sweeping the floor at

McDonald's or changing bedpans at a retirement home (another job I had in high school), if that's what it takes. I think that's important – at least for me. It's the first step toward humility, which I believe is a fundamental necessity in life. When you're starting over, the fundamentals become more important than ever.

It was time for a new mindset. Or maybe it was the revival of an old mindset. No matter—it was a different mindset.

Worksheet: Sources of Income – Sample

I started by making a list of jobs I thought I could do. I scoured the Want Ads for ideas, I talked to head hunters and temp agencies. Unfortunately, I couldn't look for full-time work because I was still trying to salvage my company and that required flexibility with my work schedule. But I could do part-time work. Some of my ideas are listed below, and I used several of them.

Consulting Work

1) instructional design
2) technical writing
3) editing
4) software training
5) eLearning

Part-Time Jobs
1) church pianist / organist
2) bartending
3) child-sitting
4) pet-sitting

Odd Jobs
1) play piano at restaurants and bars
2) teach piano lessons
3) play piano for banquets and receptions
4) real estate sales
5) Avon lady
6) Yoga instructor
7) arrange, record and sell music

Worksheet: Sources of Income – Try It!

List at least three possible jobs in each category below (more if possible). What skills do you have? Forget for the moment about whether you *like* to do the job. This is survival mode and you may have to do things you don't want to do… for awhile. For more ideas, ask your family and friends to help you brainstorm!

Full-Time Jobs
What could you do to earn a paycheck? What skills do you have? Think back to previous jobs. What have you done before? Who might want to hire you? Be specific.

1) _____
2) _____
3) _____

Part-Time Jobs
Where might you be able to find part-time work? Scan the want-ads and look at Craig's List for ideas.

1) _____
2) _____
3) _____

Odd Jobs
Think about other skills and interests. How can you use them to your advantage? Nothing is off-limits: mow yards, babysitting, pet sitting, cleaning, delivering papers, tutoring…

1) _____
2) _____
3) _____

Download this worksheet free at www.eatingramen.com.

A Different Mindset

My life had changed—almost overnight. I used to live comfortably. I didn't have to think about going out for dinner. If I wanted to go, I went, and I ordered whatever I wanted from the menu. Instant gratification. I used to buy whatever clothes I wanted. If I liked it, I bought it. Instant gratification.

At the grocery store, I used to buy whatever food looked tasty. Price was irrelevant. Toss it in the cart. Even more instant gratification. Sure, I'd see people with their coupons, working hard to save a few pennies here and there. And I would think, "Good for them!" That's where I was 20 years ago. I almost felt attached to them because I completely understood their motivation. I had been there myself. But over the years, the time it took to clip coupons gave way to other more pressing issues.

And now, here I was again. It was time to be frugal and humble. I started watching for coupons in the mail. It was time to eat what I could buy cheap, not what I had a taste for today. Small sacrifice. I picked up free local newspapers at the grocery store and looked for sales and coupons. One caution I stuck to was that I made sure I only bought things I really needed. There were loads of sales for all kinds of things that I **didn't** need. Sure, it would be nice to have a new mattress, a new microwave oven, a new desk, new luggage or new shoes. And it's the job of the advertisers to make us think we need these things. But do we? No! I had to focus only on discounts for the necessities – food, gas and personal staples like soap and deodorant. That's it.

No more designer brands. It's a complete waste of money. Marketing companies around the globe will cringe at this concept because it's how they make their living. They convince you to buy stuff that you don't really need for way too much money. Most people don't even think about it, but essentially you're paying their fee as part of the cost of whatever you're buying. Don't get me wrong: If a brand stands for quality, then being loyal to that brand has its merit. Companies like Mercedes Benz, Briggs & Riley and Levinger come to mind. Briggs & Riley gives a lifetime guarantee on their luggage because the quality is so good. No matter how your luggage is damaged, they'll repair it or replace it, even if a bus runs over it! But these companies are the exception rather than the rule.

I'm talking about the brands that make their products in Third World countries, slap their name on it and charge a fortune. My dad was a manufacturer's rep for beauty products. Back when nail polish cost 99 cents, he told me that the **real** cost of the nail polish was about 8 cents. That means we're paying more than ten times the actual cost by the time we buy it at the store. He said the designer brands were often double that, and they were exactly the same product on the inside—just the packaging was different. Why should we pay double just to have an exotic brand name on something? We're already paying ten times the actual cost to cover marketing, packaging and distribution.

There's another category of brands that I'll call celebrity brands. Some of these brands stand for nothing more than value-less living, emptiness and shallowness. Take, for example, anything with Paris Hilton's name on it. There are a host of movie stars, models and rock stars rushing to create their own brand of designer clothes, designer handbags, designer perfume, designer "anything that will sell". And plenty of it sells! Kiss founder and frontman Gene Simmons has his own line of condoms. (I do love his entrepreneurial spirit nonetheless.)   So now we're paying ten times the cost, plus double for marketing, plus another layer of padding for the people who were smart enough to come up with the idea. Does Paris Hilton really need that extra money from me? I don't think so.

Designer brands, celebrity brands...I couldn't buy designer or celebrity *anything* anymore. Unless Paris came up with her own brand of toilet paper and it was cheaper than the Walmart brand, I wasn't going to buy it.

There's a sense of humility in going into survival

mode. It means walking past the designer brands to the generic brands and buying the bare necessities, perhaps with a coupon and hopefully on sale. Here I was, the founder and president of what had until recently been a multi-million dollar company, buying generic toilet paper to save 34 cents. But then an amazing thing happened. I realized that nobody cares! One of the great things about living in a city the size of Atlanta and shopping in mega stores like Walmart is that the likelihood of being seen by anyone you know is fairly small. The cashiers aren't paying attention to what people buy—they're just doing their job. So the bottom line is: nobody knows and nobody cares.

> *My real friends didn't care whether I had Charmin or generic toilet paper in the bathroom anyway.*

At home, it occurred to me that when guests came over, I could pull out the Charmin and swap it with the generic toilet paper. Then I had another idea: *Don't invite anyone over!* Maybe it was time for me to go into a cocoon for a little while, just while I focused on Richard's mandate to stop the bleeding.

And so I did. No more entertaining. No more dinner parties. I was in hibernation mode. Sure, I kept up with my closest friends and we saw each other regularly. But we weren't going out for dirty martinis and cosmopolitans— we were staying at home and chatting over a cup of tea. My friends were simply joining me in my cocoon. My real friends didn't care whether I had Charmin or generic toilet paper in the bathroom anyway. Maybe that's the measure of true friends.

Worksheet: Mindset Changes – Sample

Here's a list of some of the mindset changes I made. It helped me to write them down and remind myself to stay committed to them.

○ I will use coupons to save money.

○ I will watch for sales, but only for necessity purchases.

○ I won't buy branded products if generic is available.

○ I won't buy any "celebrity" brand products.

○ I will pay cash for everything – no credit purchases.

○ I won't buy things on impulse for instant gratification.

○ I will constantly look for possible sources of revenue.

○ I'm not above any job or any money-saving tip.

○ It could take me years to dig out of debt (and it probably will!).

○ I'm not a lesser person because I'm broke.

○ I don't need to impress anyone.

○ My real friends could care less how much money I have.

Worksheet: Mindset Changes – Try It!

Where might you benefit from a shift in mindset? Make a list of mindset changes and share them with your family and friends. If you're like me, you may find they give you support, love – and more ideas!

- ○
- ○
- ○
- ○
- ○
- ○
- ○
- ○
- ○
- ○
- ○
- ○

Download this worksheet free at www.eatingramen.com.

Count Your Blessings

Blessings? I was hardly in the mood to think about blessings. I was in survival mode!

My personal financial statements looked like a train wreck. The stock market was in a free fall and despite my best efforts to live frugally, I was watching my brokerage account, which was leveraged to the hilt, go down, down, down.

So let's break it down. My list of assets actually wasn't that bad. I had a brokerage account, a retirement account, a business, a house, a car and oodles of "stuff" in my house. Look at all my blessings!   But there was that other column—the column of debts—that painted a starkly different picture. The business line of credit, my

> There are lots of blessings that can't be counted on a financial statement.

personal line of credit, the second mortgage on my house…the list was overwhelming at first, but no matter. I still needed to see the cold, hard facts and recognize that I owed half a million dollars more than I had to my name. Still, I could hear a little voice in the back of my head (my mom's voice?) saying: *Count your blessings.*

Then it occurred to me: There are lots of blessings that that can't be counted on a financial statement. My family, my friends, my health, my faith—these things are priceless and I had an abundance of them. So I decided to make a list of them, too. It was a different kind of asset list. I called it my Blessings Ledger, a list of things to be thankful for. I listed the names of my friends and family members—each and every one. I listed the songs I loved the most, my favorite books, my favorite movies, my favorite ice cream, my favorite quilt, my grandmother's Bible, my cat, my favorite wine. I put them all on a ledger sheet and I put it right next to the financial ledger sheet. Yes, I was still scared and I was still broke, but somehow, I was starting to feel a little bit better. Over the coming weeks and months, I added to the list as more blessings came to mind. And when I started feeling overwhelmed by my situation, I could always look at my Blessings Ledger and feel a little bit better.

I remember meeting an entrepreneur several years ago who told me his story about how he lost everything—his business, his house, his plane, his boat, his vintage cars, his life savings—all in a matter of months. He recalled crawling into bed one night in the midst of it all, and despite his large frame and seemingly strong exterior, he was reduced to tears, sobbing like a baby in a fetal position. And then he felt his wife slide in the bed behind him and put her arms around him. No words were spoken, she just held him like that until, slowly, his sobbing subsided. In the stillness of the night, with his wife's arms wrapped around him, he realized that everything that mattered to him in the world, he still had: his wife, his children, his friends, his brains, his ability to start over and build it all again. He was going to survive. Things weren't so bad after all. He counted his blessings.

I was alone in my bed that night. But my cat was curled up beside me, and her slow, steady purring was like music to my soul. I was doing the right things. I was doing the best that I could do. I was stopping the bleeding, slowly but surely. I still had a roof over my head. I had the ability and the opportunity to start over. And my Blessings Ledger was overflowing. What more could I want?!

Worksheet: Blessings Ledger – Sample

I loved creating my Blessings Ledger! And I still love looking back at it and adding more things to it. This is only a partial list...

- O Nancy C.
- O Dave Z.
- O Zemans
- O Najemniks
- O Kolars
- O Auntie Anne
- O Aunt Jenny
- O Babi
- O Dede
- O Grandpa B.
- O Brie (my cat)
- O Mozart's Requiem
- O born in USA
- O born into good family
- O Sheila A.
- O Tricia B.
- O Ann W.
- O David P.
- O Laura M.
- O born with perfect pitch
- O my church
- O my faith
- O ability to play piano
- O movie: Sound of Music
- O book: Atlas Shrugged
- O chocolate chip cookie dough ice cream
- O Handel's Hallelujah chorus
- O Steve B.
- O Daniel W.
- O beautiful sunsets
- O ice cold beer on a hot day
- O thunderstorms
- O dancing
- O buttered popcorn

- O old tapes of Saturday Night Live (original cast)
- O the first snow of winter
- O majestic mountains
- O my health
- O sense of humor
- O downhill skiing
- O the Bible
- O Jeb S.
- O Charlie B.
- O tea candles
- O yoga
- O solving puzzles
- O sitting by the fire when it's cold outside
- O sunrise over the Atlantic
- O traveling to foreign countries
- O romantic comedies
- O the French language
- O great jazz music
- O learning something new
- O laughing until I cry
- O Ken A.
- O the sound of a harp
- O Phil Collins' music
- O pasta
- O A Christmas Carol (the old black & white movie)
- O reading
- O hiking
- O the taste of red wine
- O Christmas holidays
- O Rach 2
- O freedom
- O Bing Crosby's voice

Worksheet: Blessings Ledger – Try It!

What do you have to be thankful for? Try counting your blessings to remind yourself of all the great things in your life. Use additional sheets of paper as needed.

○
○
○
○
○
○
○
○
○
○
○
○
○
○
○
○
○
○
○
○

○
○
○
○
○
○
○
○
○
○
○
○
○
○
○
○
○
○
○
○

2

Living Broke... The First Time

> *"I have learned that success is to be measured not so much by the position that one has reached in life as by the obstacles which one has overcome while trying to succeed."*

Booker T. Washington, born into slavery in 1856, became a highly respected American educator, author and spokesman for African Americans

It's Disarming to be Disowned

I was going to be a concert pianist. At the age of three, they discovered that I was born with a rare and amazing gift called perfect pitch. It meant that I could hear any sound and tell you what note it was – a horn honking, a buzzer, a bell, the melody line of a song. When my mom would practice her piano lessons and hit the wrong key, I would yell out from the next room "F sharp!" or whatever the note was supposed to be. As soon as my mom finished practicing her lessons, I would climb up on the piano bench and play every note from her lesson perfectly. It was easy for me because I knew what the notes were. This wasn't normal for such a young child, so after a pitch test at the Museum of Science & Industry in Chicago, they confirmed it: "She has perfect pitch."

And so began my path to becoming a concert pianist. My parents were elated. They loved the arts, especially music, and they desperately wanted one of their three children to be a professional musician. It appeared that I might actually have the talent to do it. I won competitions, played recitals and concerts, and I even started teaching lessons when I was 14 years old. My older brother and sister both became physicians, but that didn't seem to impress my parents as much as the possibility of me becoming a concert pianist.

Then I went off to college and majored in concert piano. My parents couldn't have been more pleased and proud. I was living their dream. But somewhere along the way, I became disenchanted with the dream. First, I never felt like I fit in at the music school. All my friends were in the Schools of Business, Science or Education. Many of the students in the School of Music seemed eccentric, reclusive or odd in some way, at least to me. Second, there was a level of competition that resulted in some cruel and dangerous pranks. To me, the most frightening prank was putting razor blades between the piano keys to injure a pianist's fingers. I always ran a text book down the keyboard before I started to practice my lessons to check for razor blades between the keys. The net result of all this was that I started struggling with nerves before a performance (something that had never happened to me before) and I lost my passion for playing the piano. And so I decided: *If this is what it's like to be a concert pianist, I don't want to be one.*

It took almost three years, until November of my junior year for me to make the final decision to end the dream. I had no idea what I wanted to do instead of being a concert pianist – my whole life had been about music up until that moment. I just knew I didn't want to be a concert pianist.

And that's how I arrived at my parents' house on Thanksgiving of my Junior year, ready to announce my decision to quit piano. And when I did, my parents disowned me. They literally kicked my tail out the front door and said I wasn't their daughter because no daughter of theirs would do such a thing. I was stunned and confused. I hitch-hiked back to college, where all my worldly goods were sitting in a tiny off-campus apartment, and I tried to figure out what to do next. It was the first time in my life that I truly had nothing. I was 20 years old.

The first thing on my mind was that I had signed a lease for my little campus apartment and I still had to pay the rent. I lost my scholarship when I dropped out of my Piano Performance major, so I needed a job. I had no experience and no real job skills to speak of. I could play a complex classical concerto and tell you what key you burped in, but that was the extent of my abilities. Neither one of them were worth much in the open job market. Being a waitress was the only thing I could think of so I applied at a restaurant and ended up with a job as a bartender. More money, better tips. It sounded good to me. I was determined never to take another penny from my parents as long as I lived. I was going to prove to them that I could be successful without their help. I didn't need them! It was the one positive aspect of a negative situation. They gave me the drive and determination to succeed against all odds.

My bartending job was at a restaurant so that was where I ate most of my meals. I remember one incident in the first few months when I had the day off. I was really hungry, but the cupboards were bare and all I had was some loose change in my purse. The rent was almost due so I couldn't afford to spend more than 30 cents on anything. I went to the grocery store and all I could

> *It was an incredibly humbling experience, but strength grew out of the adversity – the knowledge that I could survive anything.*

afford to buy was a can of corn. So I bought it and went home. Once an hour, I would eat a spoonful of corn and drink a big glass of water. That corn was delicious! And the water helped fill up my tummy. All these years later, I still remember that day. It was an incredibly humbling experience, but a kind of strength grew out of the adversity—the knowledge that I could survive anything. I had a roof over my head today, a job to go to tomorrow and the ability to pay the rent at the end of the month. So what if I was still a little hungry and sick of canned corn by the end of the day. I had made it through the day and I could do it again if I had to. There was actually a sense of pride building inside me. It was the confidence that I could survive on my own. I was going to prove to my parents that I could do just fine without them. I didn't need them or their money!

I may have been disowned, but I was a survivor—and I was determined that I was going to survive.

It Could Have Been Worse ... Much Worse

Last year, I heard Nando Parrado speak about surviving a plane crash in the Andes, where he and the other surviving passengers were stranded for 72 days. Early on, they subsisted on what little food was on the plane, watching the rations grow smaller each day. Nando said he remembered one day when each man got a ration of one peanut. He said it's amazing how you can make a single peanut last for six hours, nibbling at it one microscopic morsel at a time. Listening to his story, I remembered that day I spent with a can of corn and I felt guilty for ever thinking I had it tough. No matter where you are in life, there's always someone who's got it worse. How could I have ever felt sorry for myself? One peanut? I should have been thankful! I had a whole can of corn to myself! It's all a matter of perspective.

I believe that happiness is a choice: *Is the glass half empty or half full?* I get to choose which way I look at it, so why not choose to look on the bright side? *Of course the glass is half full!* The greatest joys in my life are my family, my friends, my health, my faith and beautiful music. Last time I checked, none of those things cost money, so even if I was broke, I could still be happy. Everything else was just gravy.

There was an article in Forbes Magazine several years

ago titled "It Could Have Been Worse... Much Worse." It poked a bit of fun at Jon Krakauer's book *Into Thin Air* which documented the saga of a bad day on Mount Everest. Indeed, eight climbers lost their lives attempting to reach the summit of Mt. Everest that day due to a combination of foul weather, poor judgment and bad luck. The point of the Forbes article was that it could have been even worse.

Take, for example, Henry Morton Stanley, the missionary and explorer who trekked thru Africa in search of Dr. Livingstone. On one of his journeys, he and more than 300 men spent three years crossing the continent, battling disease, starvation, fierce weather, hostile natives and cannibals. The 33-year old Stanley withered from 180 pounds down to 120 pounds and his hair turned white. Nearly 200 men lost their lives before they reached their destination and successfully proved the theory that Lake Victoria is the source of the Nile.

Then there was Robert Falcon Scott who attempted to lead the first expedition team to reach the South Pole. Along the way, Scott and his team suffered frostbite, snow-blindness, dehydration, scurvy and starvation among other maladies. After ten weeks and 800 miles, they finally reached the South Pole, only to find that the Norwegian team had beaten them to it. And so they began their trek back to civilization under a cloud of defeat – hopelessly weak and without sufficient supplies. Wounds refused to heal, fingernails fell off and toes turned black. The entire Scott expedition team perished over the course of the journey which lasted several months in total.

Suddenly, one bad day on Mount Everest doesn't sound so bad after all. It was only one day. And they had cell phones to call for help! Stanley and Scott had no such luxuries. Yes, it can always be worse. Respectfully remembering the difficult times that people have endured and the challenges they have overcome can be an inspiration when times are tough. Yes, I was young, broke, disowned and feeling alone in the world. But it could have been worse… much worse.

On the flip side, there's always someone who has it better than me. Oprah Winfrey

> It's a dangerous game to play – always having the latest, greatest, newest, biggest, most expensive "thing". You can never win that game.

said, "Be thankful for what you have, and you'll end up having more. If you concentrate on what you don't have, you will never, ever have enough."

There will always be someone who has more than I have. Should I compare myself to them? Should I let myself feel like a failure because the next guy has more stuff than me? Unless I'm Bill Gates, there will always be a next guy with more stuff, no matter where I am in life. Just because someone can afford a private plane and I can't doesn't mean they're better than me, more successful than me or happier than me. It doesn't mean that I should have a private plane at all. I've met people who have private planes and some of them are incredibly unhappy and/or in debt up to their ears.

It's a dangerous game to play – always having the latest, greatest, newest, biggest, most expensive "thing". You can never win that game.

I was in Omaha, Nebraska last year and I drove by billionaire Warren Buffet's house. It's a modest house in a modest neighborhood. No gates, no security guards, no attack dogs. We drove right up in the driveway and I snapped a picture of it. There's a folding chair sitting on the front porch. How normal is that? The guy gave $37 billion to charity in 2006 and he has a folding chair on the front porch of his average, middle-class house. I love that!

So I believe it's important to find the balance. I say this to put the can of corn in perspective. Someone has always got it worse. Someone has always got it better. I can't compare myself either way. I can only learn from what I see and then try to do my best. Most of all, I can be thankful for what I have and learn to be happy where I am right now. Every day. There will always be someone with more. But that's okay. There will always be someone with less. It could always be worse.

You Are Here

I always wanted to be financially secure, particularly after my parents disowned me. I didn't want to ever be dependent on anyone else like I had once been on them. Financial dependence causes people to make strange decisions, I think, and I didn't want anyone or anything to have that much control over me again. I was at a financial baseline of zero and I needed to get financially solid. But how was I going to do that? I was a scared, broke 20-year-old kid, subsisting on bartender wages. How on earth was I going to get financially secure?

After some thought, I came up with an analogy that made sense to me. I decided it's kind of like being at a mall, a museum or on campus, looking at the big map that shows you where everything is. Somewhere on that map, there's a big red "X" that says "You Are HERE". It's the starting point to get your bearings and figure out how you're going to get THERE, wherever that is.

To figure out where I stood financially (HERE), I started by making a list of everything I owned. I took a sheet of lined paper and I started writing. My list included cash balances and anything that was saleable—which was almost nothing at the time. My first list was short. I had a checking account with less than thirty dollars in it, the cash in my wallet and a bicycle. That was it. But look at my blessings! Two months before, I didn't even have that much. So this was where I stood today – my entire, financial net worth. I was at the starting line. YOU ARE HERE.

Then I needed a plan—my roadmap toward financial independence. Two things seemed critical to me. First, I needed to spend less than I earned. That was the only way I could save any money. Second, I needed to earn more. If I'm earning more, I can save even more, whereas if my income is severely limited for the rest of my life, there's a ceiling on how far I can go financially.

So I summarized my logic into a simple three-step process. I needed to:

1) Figure out where I stood financially right now, (You Are HERE),

2) Spend less money than I was earning, and,

3) Earn more money.

For inspiration, I decided to set some goals. My first major goal had three parts: 1) buy a car, 2) move into a nicer apartment, and 3) save $500. It was a huge goal for me at the time. I needed to figure out how much I needed to earn and how much I could afford to spend every month. I didn't know it at the time, but I was creating my first budget. Over the years, my budget plans would become more elaborate, more detailed and more aggressive. But they always had the same foundational principal: I needed to spend less than I earned and save a little bit every month.

> *I needed to spend less than I earned and save a little bit every month.*

Finally, I needed to stick to the plan which also meant that I needed to check my progress periodically. I decided that on the first day of the month, every month, I would update my budget list and see how I was doing. I had no idea that I was creating a simple financial statement. To me, it was just a list of numbers. I saved all the lists so that I could see my progress. I actually began to look forward to my monthly review and seeing the total at the bottom of the page go up. That's how I knew my plan was working.

Worksheet: You Are HERE – Sample

I didn't know it at the time, but my You Are HERE sheet was a Financial Statement called a Balance Sheet. The first one was practically empty, but it was a start. By subtracting "What I Owe" from "What I Own", I could see where I stood financially.

Description	Amount	Subtotal
What I Own (Assets)		
+Cash in my wallet	5.00	
+Cash in bank	27.00	
+Bicycle	25.00	57.00
What I Owe (Liabilities)		
-[Nothing]	.00	.00

My HERE Balance (Net Worth) is: $____57.00____.

Worksheet: You Are HERE – Try It!

It's easy to figure out where you stand. Just follow these easy steps.
1) List everything you own in the upper section. There are suggestions of what to include, but feel free to make changes to fit your situation.
2) List everything you owe in the lower section.
3) Subtotal each category in the right column, then subtract what you OWE from what you OWN. The result is your "You Are HERE" number!

Description	Amount	Subtotal
What I Own (Assets)		
+Cash		
+Checking Account		
+Savings Account		
+Certificates of Deposit		
+Stocks, Bonds and Other Investments		
+401K or IRA Savings		
+Life Insurance or Annuity (cash value)		
+Home (estimated value if sold today)		
+Car (estimated value if sold today)		
+Jewelry, Art, etc. (estimated value if sold today)		
+Business Ownership (estimated value if sold today)		
+Other		
What I Owe (Liabilities)		
-Home Mortgage		
-2nd Mortgage or Line of Credit		
-Car Loan		
-Credit Card Debt (card #1)		
-Credit Card Debt (card #2)		
-		

My HERE Balance (Net Worth) is: $_____.

Download this worksheet free at www.eatingramen.com.

Bony Fingers

In time, I managed to juggle three bartending jobs, all within a couple of miles from my apartment so that I could walk or ride my bike from one job to the next. If I needed to go farther, I took the bus. Within six months, I was able to put a down payment on a car. It was an old, used, beat-up blue Cutlass. I was so proud of that car! It gave me the freedom to move around on my own schedule. I could buy my groceries all at once now and not worry about buying just the two bags that I could carry in my two hands. I worked non-stop, seven days a week. Most days I worked at two of my jobs and occasionally I worked at all three of them. I didn't have time for anything else – no socializing, no TV, no dating, no church, no school. Yes, I became a college drop-out, but everything else was secondary at the moment. I just needed to make enough money to make ends meet. And I watched as the bottom line on my ledger sheet started to go up.

> Everything else was secondary at the moment. I just needed to make enough money to make ends meet.

Soon, I moved off campus into a little bigger apartment. I opened a savings account so that I could earn interest on the money I was saving. I remember when I hit $100 in my savings account, I was so happy I wanted to celebrate. And then I made a bad decision. To celebrate, I decided to buy a membership at a health club. It was a two year commitment for $19.95 per month. What was I thinking? There was a great salesman who convinced me that it was a great deal. I loved the swimming pool, the sauna and the hot tub. But I soon found they weren't worth the financial sacrifice. The payment was another noose around my neck, just like the car loan. Only I needed that car. I didn't really need the health club. In fact, I soon found that I would go for months at a time and never set foot in the health club. What a waste of money!

Over the next two years, I grew to despise that monthly payment. And I made an agreement with myself: Never again sign up for monthly payments unless I could afford to pay the entire cost up front, especially on a luxury item. Every time I look at the entire cost of something rather than the monthly payments, it'll scare me away. $19.95 a month for two years and $478.80 is the same amount of money, but $19.95 a month sure looks cheaper! Hey, maybe that's why they sell things in monthly installments! So I decided to learn from my mistake and find ways to celebrate in the future that didn't cost money. There are lots of ways to do that—take a day off, go for a long walk in the park, take a hot bath by candlelight, listen to beautiful music.

So I worked a little harder. I hired myself out to tend bar at parties. It paid a little better. And over the course of those first two years, I paid off the car. Eventually I paid off that damn health club membership, too. I remember when they asked me if I wanted to renew, I just started laughing. I had paid them $480 over the course of two years. It doesn't sound like a lot today, but it was a lot of money back then, especially to me. And what did I have to show for it? Nothing at all! What a dumb thing to pay for! At least with the car payment, I had something tangible at the end when I finally paid it off – the car!

I wanted to do something to give back, but I didn't have any spare change, so I decided to volunteer at a shelter for battered children. It was rewarding and heart-breaking all at the same time. It was another reminder that things can always be worse. I was the lucky one. My parents never beat me as a child. We didn't go for days with nothing to eat in the house except beer and potato chips. We weren't exposed to drugs, criminals and sex when we got home from school. The shelter where I worked was a one-year program for kids who came from some of the most horrible situations you could imagine. These kids were placed in the shelter due to behavioral problems. The really sad part was that at the end of the year, they had to go right back to the situation that caused the behavioral problems to begin with. It made me ten times more appreciative for my situation. I may have lost my foundation, but at least I didn't have any extreme baggage behind me or roadblocks in front of me.

Slowly but surely, I began the foundations of good money management. Some of it came from lessons my parents taught me. Some of it came by learning from my own mistakes, like the health club membership. Some of it was out of necessity and some of it was just plain common sense. Regardless of the origin, the basic principles served me well after I was disowned. Little did I know they would come in handy later in life too. Not once, but twice.

There's a great country music song with the lyrics, "Work your fingers to the bone, and what do you get? Bony fingers." I certainly had them. I also had a steadily increasing bank account and a slowly developing sense of confidence and pride.

Czech Payment Plan

Czech's are notoriously frugal. They love a bargain. In fact, they virtually demand it. They believe in working hard, living modestly and saving as much as they can. Many a Czech has gone to the grave living like a pauper with a million dollars in the bank. And while I don't necessarily plan to do that, I do believe in the underlying financial wisdom of a modest lifestyle.

My family grew up poor (and Czech) and we were always worried about money. We learned to turn out the lights when we walked out of a room. The house was always a little too cold in the winter and a little too hot in the summer. We never threw away food. Every morsel must be eaten. We had to wear our clothes until we outgrew them or they fell apart. We were taught to use only three squares of toilet paper when we went to the bathroom. We learned that you could fix almost anything with duct tape and a little WD-40. The list went on and on. No waste.

But I think the single, greatest financial lesson my parents taught me was the Czech payment plan. It goes like this: *"When you buy something, you pay 100% down… unless it appreciates in value."* Let me break that down into two parts.

Part 1: When you buy something, pay 100% down

If I buy something with 100% down, that means I have to pay cash for it. Effectively that says that if I can't afford to pay cash for something, I can't afford it. According to the Czech payment plan, that eliminates a bunch of things, like buying things on credit, using lay-away, or paying interest. Basically, it means you can't spend more money than you have. What a concept! So, how can I buy things?

What does 100% down really mean? If I'm financially responsible, I can buy things in one of four ways:

> When you buy something, pay 100% down ... unless it appreciates in value.

1) pay cash
2) write a check
3) use a debit card
4) use a credit card and pay the bill in full at the end of the month

Notice that the first three choices are all cash equivalents – the money is gone immediately. I use the term "financially responsible" because options 2 and 3 could get you in trouble if you're NOT financially responsible. Suffice it to say, I'm assuming that people would not write a bad check or use their debit card if they don't have enough money in the bank to cover the purchase. That's just plain foolish – and potentially illegal.

The fourth choice is a little different, and it requires even more financial responsibility. I can only use the credit card if I pay the bill IN FULL at the end of every month. I can't underpay the bill or I'm going to have to pay a fee, called interest and probably late charges too. That's wasted money and that's even more foolish!

If you don't quite trust yourself to be financially responsible, then stick with option 1 only – pay cash. As you start building your sense of

> If you can't afford to pay cash for something, you can't afford it.

financial responsibility, you can start moving down the list into options 2 and 3. If and when you're feeling completely confident and in complete control of your spending habits, then you can move into option 4.

Which brings me to my next point, financially responsible people can use option 4 to make money by earning interest. Here's how it works. Let's say my monthly expenses are $1,000. I can pay cash for it today, or I can put it all on my Visa card and pay for it next month when the Visa bill comes due. If I'm going to pay it in full either way, why not hold the money myself in my own interest-bearing checking or savings account? Then I can earn interest on it for an entire month, before I write the check to Visa for $1,000. So the choice is whether to write a check for the expenses now, or write a check to Visa next month. I like to earn interest on my money for as long as I can. So I charge everything I can, and I pay it in full when the bill is due. Also, I don't pay any of my bills early. I pay them right when they're due – on time and in full. So I'm earning interest on my money every single day that I possibly can, right up until I have to write the check.

Part 2: The only exception to Part 1 is if something appreciates in value

The only exception allowed in the Czech payment plan is when you buy something that increases in value over time – like real estate, fine art or antiques. Then you can use credit to purchase it, but you must be sure the cost of borrowing the money doesn't exceed the rate of appreciation. So for example, if I buy a house for $100,000 and I get a loan for $80,000 at 5% interest, I must be sure the house will appreciate at 5% per year minimum, or else I'm losing money. At the most basic calculation, my house better gain $5,000 per year in value or I can't afford to buy it.

If this doesn't make sense, listen to Dave Ramsey or find a friend who understands it and ask them to explain it.

It's an important concept. Better yet, don't buy anything on credit until you're financially stable.

Frugal Foods

When I was growing up, my dad was a traveling salesman and my mom was a stay-at-home mom. We lived in a small house that barely got us into the right school district and we had an old, beat-up car named Hildegard. Mom hand-made our clothes and I always got hand-me-downs from my sister. We never went to bed hungry, but we weren't dining like royalty. Mom bought whatever was cheap at the grocery store – calves liver, cow's tongue, ox tails – and she was a great cook so she always managed to make it taste good. If she bought a chicken, she found a way to use every part of that chicken for something. Nothing went to waste! Throwing away food was like a sin and I was sure God would strike me dead if I didn't eat every bite on my plate.

Because we were financially strapped, we didn't eat at restaurants and we didn't eat finer foods at home. I remember a delicacy food for us was black olives. We only ate two cans per year – one at Thanksgiving and one at Christmas. It was such a treat! It was as wonderful as opening a mystery Christmas present from under the tree. As a child I was fairly sure that when I grew up and I could decide what I wanted to eat for myself, I would save my money and one day I would eat an entire can of black olives all by myself!

Since I had been raised on a shoestring budget, I knew the rules of frugal eating. I knew that staples like rice and pasta were inexpensive and they could fill you up. Soup broth was another smart choice, especially as a predecessor to the main meal. Fill up on inexpensive broth so you don't eat as much of the expensive stuff that comes after. Beans and lentils are a healthy, inexpensive way to get protein – significantly cheaper than meat. They fill you up and they're full of fiber so it's a win-win. Thankfully, I loved all of these things. I could eat an entire meal of nothing but plain rice or noodles – maybe with a dab of butter and salt – and my tummy was happy. Yum!

As a twenty-year-old old kid on my own for the first time, it helped that I was small – 5 ft 1in, and I barely topped 100 pounds on the scale. It didn't take much to fill my tummy!

I experimented with ways to take inexpensive foods and stretch them out. I invented poor man's French onion soup – put a piece of bread in the bottom of a bowl, add sautéed onions and two scoops of cottage cheese, then pour beef broth on top. Yum. I revived one of my mom's old mainstays that she called Sala Magundy – sautée 1 onion, 3 peppers and 6 tomatoes. Scoop them over macaroni and you have a low cost meal. Yum.

I also enjoyed making what I called spaghetti soup. It

was simply beef broth and pieces of broken spaghetti noodles. In retrospect, I was an inventor, creating an archaic version of Ramen soup – something I had never heard of before. I liked it plain, but I also liked experimenting with different broths and different spices. Sometimes I would add a vegetable or two, like celery, carrots or onion, diced in small bits so as not to overshadow the pasta.

Imagine my joy years later when I discovered ramen noodle soup at the grocery store. It was incredibly cheap with a variety of flavorings. And it took me back to my survival days, young adulthood. It was a time when I was terrified of what the future might

Imagine my joy years later when I discovered ramen noodle soup at the grocery store.

hold and at the same time excited by the possibilities of the unknown. Every day was an adventure. Kind of like the first day of school – You didn't know whether to be happy or afraid, you didn't know if it would be a good year or a bad year, you didn't know if your teacher would be a kind, supportive, pretty lady or a mean witch. The stakes were bigger in the game of life than in the first grade, but I was equally clueless about what would happen next.

I can't even guess how many times I have heard people say that the difficult years were the best years of their life.

For me too, the process of struggling through challenges was often the best part. Coming out whole and strong on the other end is the goal, the final prize. But the journey to get there can be far more rewarding than the prize itself. Ramen noodles always take me back to that journey. It's like a secret, added ingredient, hidden from the Nutrition label, and it makes them taste just a little bit better. Yum!

In the early days, my best source of food was at the restaurants and bars where I worked. But there were times when I wasn't working, or I just couldn't stomach another cheeseburger, or I didn't have enough money to buy groceries. That's when some of the alternative foods came in handy.

Alternative Foods

When I was little, my parents chose NOT to teach us how to speak Czech. They were both first generation Americans and they didn't learn to speak English until they went to grade school. They said they always felt like they were second class Americans as a result and they didn't want us to feel the same way. They wanted us to feel like we were pure Americans. So we learned a few choice phrases in Czech, but not enough to converse. I could count to ten, say "Good night, I love you" and "you pooped in your pants." These are important phrases when you're two years old. But that was about the extent of my vocabulary, except for one very important word. "Houbi." Houbi translates to mushroom in English. I knew it well because houbi is a staple in the Czech diet. In fact, we used to go "houbi hunting" as a family outing and we ate houbi all year long.

Houbi hunting was most popular in the summer and fall. We would all pile into the car and drive to Kickapoo State Park in central Illinois, each person armed with a brown paper bag. It was a race to see who could get the most houbi in their bag. My parents taught us what to look for in good mushrooms – the color, the texture, the size. You have to be very careful because some houbis are poisonous! My brother, sister and I would get distracted and play all kinds of games in the woods so our bags were usually half full, but my mom and dad were serious houbi hunters. Sometimes they would fill several large brown grocery bags full of houbi. We would drive home and mom would spread out all the little treasures on the kitchen counter. She would inspect them to be sure they weren't rotted or poisonous, then she proceeded to dry them or freeze them and make them into delicious dishes like houbi soup, houbi salad and houbi meatloaf. Great stuff! Free food!

I was 20 years old now and it was time to go Houbi Hunting on my own. So I grabbed a brown paper bag and headed out to the woods. Parks, meadows, fields – they were all potential breeding grounds for houbi. I found plenty of other treats in my path too – berries, nuts and fruits. As long as there were no signs posted to stop me, I helped myself. Free food!

I have always been an animal lover, and one day I found a stray kitten behind my apartment. She was a calico cat, just like the one I had as a little girl and I couldn't very well leave her out there in the elements to survive on her own. I named her Charmin, like the toilet paper. "Please don't squeeze the Charmin, Mr. Whipple."

I remember coming home from work one night after I had worked a double shift and I was exhausted. My feet were throbbing and my back hurt from lifting a beer keg. I walked in the door, dropped everything on the floor and plopped down in the middle of the hallway in a heap. I didn't even turn the light on – I just sat there in the dark for several minutes, letting my poor feet rest. Charmin climbed up in my lap and started purring. I was hungry but I was too tired to get up and cook anything, and I knew there wasn't much in the pantry anyway.

And that's when I realized that Charmin's food bowl was within reach. *Hmmm... I wonder what cat food tastes like.* And so I reached over, grabbed a piece of Little Friskies and popped it in my mouth. Crunchy, a little bit salty, kind of like a cross between a pretzel, a nut and liver sausage. Not too bad. I decided it would taste better with a Miller Lite and I was right. So that's what I had for dinner that night – Miller Lite and Little Friskies. I munched on

> Crunchy, a little bit salty, kind of like a cross between a pretzel, a nut and liver sausage. Not too bad.

my gourmet feast with pride. It was certainly inexpensive!

And then, there was garbage. Well, not really. It's just that so many people leave perfectly good food behind as garbage. Even supposedly poor college students. Occasionally, I would go to one of the campus cafeterias and sit near the racks where people would take their trays after they had finished eating. I would watch for trays that had untouched food – like a whole fried chicken breast or a whole apple. I'd wait until they walked away and when I thought nobody was looking, I'd take my tray up and grab whatever was on their tray. To this day, I don't know if anyone noticed what I was doing. At the time, I thought I was pretty discreet and I was totally sure I got away with it. But who knows… And, in fact, who cares. It was survival.

At the bars and restaurants where I worked, we'd carry customers' plates back to the kitchen and snarf up unused food that the customers didn't want. We couldn't re-serve it to someone else so we had to either throw it away or eat it. As long as I was relatively sure the customer hadn't touched the food, I was happy to eat it. I never went dumpster diving, but I would have if it had come to that. It's amazing what you'll do when you're hungry and broke.

The "Little" Great Depression

My parents grew up during the Great Depression of the 1930s and it obviously scarred them for life. To this day, they can't tolerate throwing away a single bread crumb. I can't imagine what it must have been like, but I heard the stories growing up. Now that I was on my own, I was suffering through my own Little Great Depression. I remembered some of their stories and I put several of them to use:

Tips from the Great Depression

- Hand-make your clothes. Repair rips and seams. Patch up holes. Darn your socks. Wear it until you outgrow it.
- When the clothes are too ripped up to wear or repair, cut them into pieces and make a quilt.
- When all your kids outgrow their clothes, find a neighbor with smaller kids and give them your clothes. It's like a windfall for them!
- Don't wear shoes in the summer. Go barefoot.
- Eat everything on your plate. Never throw food away. If you are truly so full that you can't eat any more, save the rest for later, but don't throw it away!

- Save the water when you boil vegetables and use it as basic broth for soups and stews. It's tasty... and healthy too!

- Save the grease when you're cooking meats and use it to cook other things – eggs, fish, potatoes, stew.

> *Save the water when you boil vegetables and use it as basic broth for soups and stews. It's tasty... and healthy too!*

- Save leftover meat and vegetables all week and throw them all into a pot roast on Friday. Yummy!

- Feed the children the healthiest possible food. Let the adults eat the bad stuff and/or go to bed hungry.

- If you're negligent enough to let food spoil before you eat it, use the rotten food as bait to catch other critters to eat – fish, rabbits, squirrels, etc.

- To save money on meat, buy whatever the butcher has marked down for last day sale – and cook it today!

- Save aluminum foil, baggies, paper bags, straws, foam cups, bread bags cereal bags, etc. Re-use them all until they literally fall apart.

- Save lidded glass jars (from peanut butter, jams, olives, etc.). Re-use them for storage of food, nails, thumb tacks, whatever.

- Forget paper towels. Use cloth rags that can be washed out and re-used.

- Forget toilet paper. Pages from the local newspaper or the Sears catalog work just fine.

- Start a garden and grow your own vegetables. Grow your own spices too. Don't buy something at the store if you can grow it yourself.

- Use dandelion greens on your salad to add flavor. It's an alternative spice.

- Start a compost pile with leftover foods, then use it for fertilizer in the garden.

- Always check gas prices. Prices can vary a lot from one gas station to the next. Always keep an eye out, whether you need gas or not, so that when you do need it, you'll know exactly where to go – and not waste more gas looking!

- Make toys for the kids instead of buying them at the store. It requires creativity and lets the imagination run free. For example, make a doll out of a corn cob, sticks, fabric strips and yarn scraps.

- Make your own fly swatter with a stick and some screen wire from old torn-up window screens.

- For note paper, use the back of envelopes and paper that has printing on only one side.

- Bury your money in fruit jars (water-tight seal) in the back yard where the banks can't get to it and the robbers can't find it.

- Squeeze every ounce out of the toothpaste tube and empty every container of liquid until it's bone dry before you throw it away.
- Work multiple jobs – both parents. The kids have to pitch in around the house because the parents are too tired from all the work outside the home.
- Put your kids to work doing odd jobs for hire – mowing yards, doing laundry, babysitting, even hard labor if an employer will hire them.
- Give gifts that don't cost money. Write little IOU notes for things like "20-minute back rub" or "30-minute walk in the park" or "5 free music lessons". Wrap up the notes and you have a free gift.

There are a million of these tips. In the Great Depression, people were trying to survive. Food, shelter and clothing were the top priority, and for many people – the only priority. The fact that everyone was in it together probably made it more terrifying (will it ever end, who will win the war, will we ever be normal again?) and more comforting (at least everyone else is suffering too – neighbors, friends, family) all at the same time.

I was in my own private "Great Depression", all by myself. So I used as many of these little pearls of wisdom as I could. Everything had multiple uses. Almost nothing went in the trash if I could figure out another way to use it productively. The recycling craze hadn't started yet, but I was recycling like crazy – all by myself, for myself, in my own little apartment.

My Piggy Bank

I remember when I was little, I had a piggy bank. So did my brother and sister, and we compared our piggy bank balances periodically. My brother was always the winner, although it was mildly irritating that he didn't seem to care. Maybe it was all an act to get my goat because I did care. I would have loved to win that race! He grew up to have excellent money management skills – paying off his car, his house and his med school loans before he turned 40. He has lived debt free ever since. Shortly after his two daughters were born, he established a fund for each of them. Their personalities were like night and day and he joked that they had a college fund for Lisa and a bail fund for Haley. It nearly came true.

I think the biggest lesson I learned from the piggy bank was to save, save, save. We didn't have a lot of opportunity to earn money as kids, so there wasn't much to save. We were poor enough that we didn't get an allowance, so we had to rely on gifts from relatives at Christmas, the tooth fairy (10 cents per tooth), and our semi-annual report card (25 cents for each A). When we were old enough, we had a lemonade stand, mowed yards and babysat for the neighbors. My parents provided food, shelter and clothing. But everything else was a luxury. We never dared ask for anything else. If you wanted something, you had to save for it and buy it yourself. As a child, I didn't realize how much food, shelter and clothing cost. I'm sure my parents had a tough time making ends meet on my dad's salary alone. But at the same time, we all took music lessons. So my

> *I completely abandoned the idea of vacations. If I wasn't working, I wasn't earning money, so it didn't seem logical.*

parents obviously decided where they wanted to invest what little extra they had, and that was in music. (No wonder they were so mad at me when I decided to quit!)

I remember going on only three family vacations when I was growing up. We couldn't afford much so they were camping vacations. We had a vacation piggy bank that was used to save for the vacation. I remember once a week we would all gather around the pink piggy bank, open the pig's tummy and count everything inside. Each week, the balance would go up a little bit, although in retrospect, I don't remember where the money came from. In their own way, my parents were teaching us that you have to save for things you want. And it can take a very long time to get there.

As an adult on my own, I completely abandoned the idea of vacations. If I wasn't working, I wasn't earning money, so it didn't seem logical to take a vacation. Having been disowned, I didn't have a family to visit on the holidays anyway, so I was happy to fill in and work for people who actually had somewhere to go. I found that keeping busy was not only a great way to earn money and pay the bills, it also kept me busy enough that I didn't have time to feel sorry for myself. No pity party for me; in fact, I was quite cheerful about the fact that I was getting along so well. Over time, I was invited to other people's holiday gatherings and I was thankful for that. The glass was more than half full.

My adult piggy bank was a savings account, earning interest on every penny. I loved to see the balance going up. Someone told me once that you should have six months of living expenses in your savings account. That way, if you lose your job, you can live like a normal person for six months while you're looking for another job. It made good sense to me, so that was my next savings goal. Six months of expenses.

Another one of the lessons from my dad was that you have to track every penny. You have to see where your money is going and you have to do it on a regular, timely basis. If you wait too long, you may not find out you're in trouble until it's too late to fix it. I got in the habit of balancing my checkbook every month, right after my bank statement arrived. I always knew where I stood financially. Each month, I looked at where I spent my money, down to the penny. Having to write it down raised my awareness and I've continued the practice to this day.

Buy Quality

Now this one may sound counter-intuitive at first. Doesn't quality cost money? I didn't have any money, so why would I want to spend more of what I didn't have? But there are two underlying principles that are worth consideration.

First, good quality lasts longer. Let's take a simple pair of pants. Buy a cheap pair of pants and they rip easily, the seams wear out, the buttons pop off, they fray, they get fuzz balls, the wrinkles won't come out, the stains won't come out and pretty soon they just look old and nasty. The Salvation Army wouldn't want them.

Now, take a high quality pair of pants. They could last for years. This, of course, means you must buy more timeless styles when you buy the quality pair since they're going to last so long. A quality pair of bell-bottom blue jeans has a limited shelf life due to the style. But make careful, timeless choices and you can wear them for years.

I was traveling in India last year and I fell on the street. I simply lost my balance and in an instant, I toppled forward onto my knees – hard! The pain was excruciating. I didn't even know this was possible, but I had split open my left leg right below the knee cap – all the way to the bone in a jagged tear. I had to have emergency surgery in Bombay. No fun. But, here's the amazing part. I was wearing a pair of pants when I fell. And the pants didn't even rip! My knee ripped apart to the bone, but my pants stayed intact. I washed the blood out and wore those pants again a week later. Now that's quality!

And it's not just about clothes. Buy quality everything – furniture, accessories, home appliances, cars. If you MUST buy something, be sure it's quality! Let me tell you about my desk – my favorite desk....

I saw the most beautiful desk in the world at a Scandinavian furniture store. It was solid teak and it cost $1500. In the late 70's, that was a small fortune – especially to me. Yes, I could have bought it on credit, but that wouldn't be on the Czech Payment Plan. It would be instant gratification on a credit card. So instead, I started saving for that desk. It took me over three years to save the money – on top of my regular saving goals. But I did it. I was so proud to walk into the store and write a check for my desk. (I learned later that I probably could have asked for a cash discount, but I didn't know to do that at the time.) I wrote the check and they delivered my desk. That was

> It's better to buy nothing than to buy something cheap.

over 20 years ago and to this day, I have that desk and I use it daily. It's a beautiful, honey-colored, solid teak desk with curved edges and a spacious desktop. It has moved with me across the country, to the office, back to the house, back to the office again and back to the house again. It still looks like new and it's solid as a rock. Great quality. Great investment.

The second point about quality is this. If you can't afford quality, you can't afford it. So don't buy it at all. It's better to buy nothing than to buy something cheap. Keep eating on the floor if you can't afford a good quality kitchen table. You'll appreciate the kitchen table so much more when you finally get it. And for God's sake, don't charge it. Remember the Czech payment plan!

Oh, by the way, don't think that a high price tag equates to good quality. Sometimes the opposite is true. Is it frugal or is it cheap – be sure you know the difference. Look for sales. Going out of business sales are more common in a down economy. Do the math. Remember that instant gratification is your enemy.

Save well. Buy quality. Pay cash.

Tips from Auntie Anne

As a kid, one of my favorite relatives was dear, old Auntie Anne. She wasn't really my aunt, she was my godmother, but we grew up calling her Auntie Anne. She was one of the funniest people in the world and we loved her dearly. As a little kid, I loved visiting her because she made everyone laugh. Most Czech's are kind of grumpy. But not Auntie Anne. She was the jolliest lady around.

In addition to her sense of humor, I think Auntie Ann might have been the most frugal person ever – the original, quintessential miser, the queen of all penny pinchers. She knew no boundaries, and she was probably laughing all the way to the bank. She REALLY

> If it wasn't bolted down, Auntie Anne believed it was free for the taking.

knew how to pinch a penny. And if it wasn't bolted down, Auntie Ann believed it was free for the taking. There's a very funny Czech movie called "The Fireman's Ball". It's in Czech and it's all about the Czech culture so most people probably wouldn't appreciate it much. But there's one scene that anyone could appreciate in any language. An old woman at a big party takes a rump roast off the banquet table and sneaks it into her over-sized purse. The roast wasn't bolted down, so it must be free! It's classic. I wouldn't be surprised if Auntie Anne lifted a rump roast or two in her day too.

Okay, I'm not necessarily recommending Auntie Anne's strategies. But in honor of my dear old Auntie Anne, and for those who are really desperate, here's the cheapest of the cheap:

- Never buy condiments. Go to any fast food restaurant and help yourself to packets of salt, pepper, straws, stir sticks, ketchup, mustard, taco sauce, even napkins.
- Don't buy fancy condiments either. On the rare occasion when you eat at a real restaurant, go to the ones that put condiments right on the table – butter, jelly, honey, etc. – in nice little packets or miniature jars that fit nicely into your purse.
- Don't buy magazines. Just pick some up at the doctor's office next time you're in for a visit.
- Never buy toilet paper. There are rolls sitting around all over the place – at restaurants, doctor's offices, office buildings, hotels, even on airplanes. Worst case – use the free napkins from McDonald's.
- When you stay at a hotel, there are all kinds of freebies – soap, notepaper, pens, shampoo, lotion, sewing kit, etc. In some hotels, you can even ask the front desk for a razor, toothbrush, toothpaste or comb and they'll give you one. Free!

- Always bend down to pick up loose change on the street. It's amazing how much is there if you just look for it. There are lots of great places, like – the check-out lane at the grocery store, any place that has a cash register and toll booths. (Today, check out the security lane at the airport.) Throw it all in a special jar and see how fast it adds up.

- Don't sit down to eat at a restaurant. Order take-out and pick it up. You save the tip for the server.

- Some restaurants have a lunch menu and a dinner menu. Even if it's dinner time, ask if you can order off the lunch menu. It's cheaper and sometimes, you get the same amount of food. And even if the portions are smaller on the lunch menu, who needs the extra calories?

- Do you ever get a letter where the stamp hasn't been postmarked? Steam it off and glue it on your own letter. Free stamps!

- It's not just wrapping paper that is re-usable. Bows and ribbons are too. Don't tear into a gift like a baboon. Remove everything carefully, fold it neatly, and save it all for someone else's gift next time around.

- Re-use the same card. Auntie Ann and Uncle Bob gave each other the same Anniversary Card every year, for over 40 years, until the day he died.

- Use plain paper bags for wrapping paper, get some markers and crayons and draw your own design!
- Don't throw away used Baggies. Wash them out, hang them over a bottle to dry and use them again.
- If you're not 100% satisfied with a purchase, return it and raise hell until they give you your money back.
- If you're at a restaurant and you don't like the food, complain until they take it off the check. Never settle for mediocre!

Auntie Anne was so proud of me for being an entrepreneur. She was born in the early 1900s, but if she had been born a few years later, I'm sure she would have been an entrepreneur herself. She would have crushed the competition too, whatever her business was! Her wit, her humor and her energy were unstoppable.

No, she didn't make pretzels – that's a different Auntie Anne. My Auntie Anne lived in a small house in La Grange, Illinois. As a young lady, she worked as a secretary at Western Union, married Uncle Bob, and moved into a house with a white picket fence. I remember they used to take separate vacations – Auntie Anne would travel all over the world and at the same time, Uncle Bob would go on a fishing trip with his buddies. It worked for them. They never had any children and Uncle Bob died of lung cancer in the 1960's. Auntie Anne lived another 40 years. She died in her 90's, in the same little house with the white picket fence. When I close my eyes and picture her, I see her laughing. Then I look at her hand and I see her pinching a penny. Thanks for the lessons, Auntie Anne – and the laughs!

A Thanksgiving Attitude

Thanksgiving is a holiday of special meaning to me. Yes, it marked the day when I was disowned by my parents all those years ago. But from a positive perspective, it was the day my parents handed me a great gift – the gift to believe in myself and learn that I was a survivor. Determination and commitment to achieve a goal are amazingly powerful tools.

I get to choose how I look at everything that happens in my life and I choose to look at being broke as a blessing. Every Thanksgiving for the past 30 years, I remember what it was like to be penniless, starting out with nothing, scared and alone. It was humbling. It grounded me. But the best part was that I had my entire life ahead of me. My life was a blank slate. I could turn it into whatever I wanted it to be. I believe my parents gave me that gift too – the power to believe I could do anything, even build a multi-million dollar company, travel the world and someday be able to give back more to others than I once had myself. It was only going to get better from there.

Norman Vincent Peale wrote a great, timeless book called *The Power of Positive Thinking*. The book is full of stories, including one about two brothers – one is an alcoholic, and the other one never drinks. Mr. Peale met the first brother and asked him why he was an alcoholic, and he replied (and I paraphrase) "Of course, it's because my father was an alcoholic". Mr. Peale then met the second brother and asked him why he never drank, and he replied "Of course, it's because my father was an alcoholic." We are all dealt a hand in life, and indeed some people are dealt a better hand than others, but it's what we do with that hand that matters. It's our choice.

Thank God for Thanksgiving. It's a great time for me to do an attitude check, remember that millions of other people in this world are suffering, and be thankful for every blessing I've been given.

I started something years ago that has become a daily habit for me. It keeps me in the Thanksgiving frame of mind. Each night when I crawl into bed, I think of ten things from the day that I can be thankful for. For example:

- *I'm thankful because I visited with an old friend.*
- *I'm thankful because I got a phone call with good news.*
- *I'm thankful because it was a beautiful day with lots of sunshine.*
- *I'm thankful because I saw a funny movie tonight.*
- *I'm thankful because one of my all-time favorite songs was on the radio while I was driving home.*

They don't have to be big and important things. They can be small nuggets of something that was good if only because it wasn't bad. Some days the list is easy and I zip up to 10 things in a minute. Other days, I find myself struggling to get to 10, and on those days, I can reach into my timeless list. I'm thankful for my health. I'm thankful that I have a roof over my head. I'm thankful that I was born in the United States of America.

A friend and mentor once told me, the only real problems in this world are the ones that money can't solve. Think about it. Can money solve a terminal disease? No, and that makes it a real problem. Anything less is just an annoyance. Every so often, we hear about the death of a person who was fabulously famous or incredibly rich. It doesn't matter how rich and famous you are when you're terminally ill. Money can't solve it. Being rich and famous can't fix it. It's a REAL problem because it's going to get you no matter what.

> *The only real problems in this world are the ones that money can't solve.*

When you're facing something like that, all the other things that you thought were a problem don't seem like real problems anymore. It's all a matter of perspective.

The truth is, in fact, life is terminal. From the minute we're born, we know we're going to die. A 98-year old woman once told me "None of us are getting out of this alive!" I laughed and so did she. But at the end of the day she was right, of course. So we can look at life as a death sentence and live under a cloud of doom, or we can look at every day as a blessing, the story between the bookends, and enjoy each day of the story to its fullest. I get to choose and I choose to enjoy each day as a blessing.

So I was a bartender for about a year when I was promoted to bar manager. Another year later and I got my first "real" job, working with computers at a construction company. Then I got a job with a software company teaching accountants how to put their financial records on computer. A few years later, I decided to start my own business, teaching people how to use computers. Then I got married. As a wedding present, my husband gave me a piano. My blessings were piling up. I may have been disowned, but I was surviving just fine.

3

Till Divorce Do Us Part

> *"Whether you think you can
> or you think you can't,
> you are right."*

Henry Ford, Founder of the Ford Motor Company,
father of the modern assembly line
used in mass production

Unholy Matrimony

Marriage was great. I was just married to the wrong guy. He was a good guy in a lot of ways. We just went through a string of bad events – miscarriage, family deaths, three hurricanes in one year, two car accidents, our dog died. It was like a bad country music song.

We were great together during the good times, but we stunk together during the bad times. I really wasn't happy and if I hadn't left I'm afraid I would have regretted it later – wondering if there was something else, something better or more fulfilling. Should I have "settled" and stayed with him? Well, it doesn't matter much to think about it now. We've both moved on with our lives and I choose to look forward instead of looking back. We had a few good years together and I'm thankful for that. We had a few lousy years and that's why I left. End of story.

I always thought I would get married once and only once. (Actually, that may come true if I don't meet the right guy soon!) At the time I got divorced, I was the one who wanted out so I was willing to give up anything and everything to get out of the relationship. All I took with me were my piano, my desk, my clothes and my cat. I had less than $300 in the bank. That was it. I didn't even have a car. I had sold my car when we got married and we bought another car together. It was a Mercedes 300D, purchased on a note that only charged us interest, but we never paid a penny on the principal. I didn't want a car with that kind of deal!

Money was a fundamental point of disagreement in our marriage. He liked to spend it. I liked to save it. He liked to buy things on credit. I liked to pay cash. He liked to gamble. I saw gambling as a tax on people who are really bad at statistics. To me, buying a car and paying interest only – no principal – was about as far away from the Czech Payment Plan as you could get. So after the divorce, I chose to buy my own car on terms that I could live with. I couldn't buy a car for $300 cash, so I had to break my own rule of 100% down and get a loan. Ouch! But I had a plan to pay it off in a year. And I did. It was a big step down from a Mercedes 300D. It was a Chevrolet Celebrity, a clunky 4-door, boxy silver car like your grandmother would drive. It wasn't beautiful, it wasn't sexy, it wasn't as sturdy as the Mercedes, but it got me where I wanted to go... in more ways than one.

So here I was again, starting over with next to nothing – no savings, no roof over my head, no car. Thankfully, I had a good credit rating so I was able to rent a small, run-down house in a semi-rough neighborhood. It was a far cry from the beach-front house where my husband remained with the swimming pool in the back yard, upper class neighbors and beautiful views of the bay. It turned out I wasn't alone when I moved into my new home. It was also home to a million cockroaches – not just the little, dirty, nasty ones that scurry around really fast, but the great big palmetto bugs that are as big as your fist. It was gross and it was humbling. I was truly starting over again.

Divorce was a painful experience. Even though I was the instigator, it still hurt like hell. So to numb the pain, I buried myself in work. It served multiple purposes. It kept me busy, it kept my mind off the pain and it helped

> *I buried myself in work. It kept me busy, it kept my mind off the pain and it helped me re-build my bank account.*

me re-build my bank account. Within a matter of months, I found a rent-controlled apartment that didn't have cockroaches. Me, my cat and my Chevrolet Celebrity moved in as fast as we could. I was an independent consultant and I provided corporate training and curriculum development. It paid pretty well and since I was willing to work double shifts, it paid REALLY well!

Once again, I reverted to the same three steps:

1) Figure out where I stood.

2) Spend less than I earned.

3) Earn more.

And so I did. Within a year, I paid off the car, I was

building my savings account and I was getting enough business that I had to hire a contractor to help me. Thankfully, I continued my frugal ways and refined my activities and routines to match my budget. After a failed marriage fraught with really bad money management techniques, it felt really good to 'Get Smart' with money again.

Smart Living

There were some basic things I did right away to help with the utility bills. I was living in Atlanta so the summers were hot and humid. I avoided turning on the air-conditioner at all costs. Only when my little apartment turned into a veritable sauna did I give in – and that was only a handful of times during the summer. I used small fans so that I could keep the A/C usage to a minimum, and I kept a spray bottle nearby to spritz myself periodically. It made the fan feel even cooler.

At home, I dressed light – shorts and a tank top or swimsuit. I always had a fan blowing on me. During the day whether I was at home or not, I kept the window shades down to keep the sunlight from heating up the inside. They hadn't invented reflective coatings for windows yet, but someone told me to put aluminum foil on the windows to block even more light. I guess that was the predecessor to

> I tried aluminum foil on the windows but it made my apartment look like a prison from the outside and it felt like a cave on the inside.

window coatings. I tried it for a while, but it made my apartment look like a prison from the outside and it felt like a cave on the inside, so I searched for alternatives. I checked the windows and doors for leaks, sealing them up with duct tape. Sometimes it still felt like a sauna so I continuously looked for more ideas.

I kept chores to a minimum, avoiding tasks that involved appliances – like cooking. I bought a little hibachi grill that I could use on my porch to cook things outside rather than heating up the oven or the stove inside. I kept the TV and the lights off as much as possible. They all generate heat and I was feeling sluggish enough as it was.

On the rare occasion when there was a cool evening and a nice breeze, I would open the windows to let in the cool air. I slept in a room that didn't get direct sunlight and there were plenty of trees shading the window, so it was the coolest room in the house.

I ate light and I drank lots of fluids to keep hydrated. I stayed away from alcohol and caffeine products – both will dehydrate your body and that can cause heat stress. Fresh fruits and frozen fruit treats are a great snack to stay cool. Salads were a fresh, light meal. I added nuts, cheese, veggies and cold-cuts to make it a well-balanced meal.

During the day, I was in office buildings so it was easy to stay cool in their air conditioning. Sometimes I would bring my dinner to the office and work late just to eat in the cool temperatures. Other nights, I would venture out to the mall, the library or the bookstore to read or work in the air conditioning -- their air conditioning. Somebody else was paying the bill anyway, why shouldn't I enjoy it? I met some nice people at the library and there was a great selection of books – all for free! It kept me busy and it kept me cool. I tried not to do much of anything except sleep when I was at home.

In the winter, the challenges were reversed. Yes, it gets cold in Atlanta – down to the 20's and 30's. It usually snows once or twice a year but it rarely sticks for more than a few minutes. But due to the humidity, the cold weather in Atlanta feels REALLY cold.

I used some of the basic summertime techniques in reverse. On sunny days, I opened the shades to let the sunlight pour in thru the windows. The windows weren't double pane so I got poster board and cut it to the size of the window. I would put the poster boards up at night, two or three sheets per window, for added insulation. It was much cheaper than drapes, and since I was in a rental apartment, I wasn't interested in buying drapes or blinds.

Window and door leaks were easier to detect in the winter and I sealed them up with duct tape. I also enjoyed taking a hot bath for a treat. I figured it cost money to generate the hot water, but I always felt warmer and slept better on nights after I had a warm bath. I also enjoyed double benefit activities like exercising. It was healthy for me and I could work up a sweat. I stayed warm for nearly an hour after a good workout.

In the winter, my food choices leaned toward soups which were inexpensive and warmed me up on the inside. Adding a variety of vegetables, beans, barley or rice made it healthy and experimenting with spices made it taste good. I drank plenty of hot tea and sometimes I would drink plain hot water. People drink cold water, and room-temperature water. Why not drink hot water? When you're cold on the outside, it's warm and soothing on the inside – and it's good for you too.

In the evenings and on weekends, I ventured out to the mall, the bookstore, even to church to find a warm place to thaw out. There was a Methodist church fairly near my apartment – within walking distance. I used to go to the sanctuary and play piano in the evenings. It was toasty warm there and their piano was in better shape than mine. Thankfully, the people at the church didn't seem to mind.

I wore layers to stay warm, and I always had on a hat or ear muffs when I was outside. I slept with lots of layers on my body and layers of blankets on my bed. My cat was like a little space heater under the blankets. It was a "three-dog night" and I only had one cat, but I made the best of it!

Smart Shopping

Thankfully, I've never been a big shopper or a big spender, probably because of the way my parents raised me. The only stores where I can get into really big trouble are bookstores and music stores. While I was married, my shopping habits became more lax, probably from my husband's influence, but I mostly stuck to the Czech Payment Plan. He didn't do the same but at least he liked quality. Unfortunately, he was into designer labels and I had to gulp when he would spend $200 on a pair of Ray-Ban sunglasses. Who needs that? I guess he knew he looked good in his Ray-Bans, driving the bank's Mercedes!

After the divorce, things were different and I had to make some changes. I can classify the changes to my shopping habits into three categories: Timing, Planning and Discounts.

Timing

I limited my grocery shopping to once a week. This forced me to plan and it reduced the urge to buy on impulse. I shopped for groceries on Saturday night to avoid the crowds. I had two stops – the open air market, where I would buy fresh, local produce at great prices, and the regular grocery store where I would buy everything else. It's actually quite pleasant shopping at the grocery store on

Saturday night when the aisles are empty. No long lines at check-out. No screaming children running around. It's calm and serene.

All other shopping except grocery shopping, I limited to once a month. That meant clothes, books, electronics, appliances, furniture, etc. – anything that I couldn't buy at the grocery store. If I felt an urge to run out and buy something, I asked myself if I absolutely, positively had to have it RIGHT now. Was it something I really needed right now, or was it just instant gratification. Funny thing – never once did I have to have it RIGHT now. Apparently, I had been buying lots of things for instant gratification. But now, after really thinking about it for a few minutes, I became aware that I didn't really NEED to have it. I would write whatever it was on the monthly shopping list and continue on with my day. Then, and this is very important, I would go on my monthly shopping excursion and I would ONLY buy the things that were on my monthly list. No impulse buys, no temptations. Just walk into the store, buy what was on the list, and leave. I can't begin to estimate how much money I saved with these timing habits.

Planning

I planned my meals for the week. No impulse buys at the grocery store either! I wrote out what I planned to eat, day by day. That included brown bag lunches at the office, which are a huge savings over eating out. Then I made my grocery list. I always had a list when I went shopping

> When you're hungry, lots of things hop into your grocery cart that don't need to be there.

because without it, I was a spending binge waiting to happen. And I learned not to go to the grocery store right before a meal. When you're hungry, lots of things hop into your grocery cart that don't need to be there. Eat a big meal, and THEN head to the grocery store to do your grocery shopping.

It became a little game for me to try to spend a little less each week than the week before. I found myself digging into the pantry and eating up things that had been hiding in there for way too long – canned goods, oatmeal, rice, un-opened boxes of whatever. I never digressed to the cat food, but I was amazed at how much food was just sitting there in boxes and cans, waiting to be eaten. With a bit of creativity, I devised recipes to devour the food. Soups and salads were a favorite way of mixing together unlikely ingredients. I could toss almonds and water chestnuts into my salad, or add barley and lentils to my soup. Delicious!

I always checked out the local farmer's market for fresh produce. Many times they're cheaper because the middle man is gone. It's a great way to get good, healthy food at a lower price. I wanted to eat healthy, but I was also keen on finding foods that were inexpensive. And that's when I made my best food discovery of the century. Ramen noodles! One package makes a meal, and in the late 80's, a package cost about 10 cents. That's an entire meal for 10 cents! During the first few months after my divorce, I ate ramen noodles almost daily as a meal. You could dress them up with different spices for variety (and today there are lots of different flavors off-the-shelf) so I never really got tired of it.

Discounts

My third change was to become a coupon queen. This, I learned, was an art form and there are entire books (and websites today) devoted to it. I will never look down my nose at someone shuffling thru their coupons at the grocery store. I know now how important every penny can be and I know I can save a boatload of pennies with coupons. Some stores even offer a double coupon day where you get twice the value of the coupon back.

Also, I always picked up the flyer on in-store specials to watch for non-perishables that I could buy and stock up on. Better to buy them on special than wait until I run out and pay full price.

Postscript

Even after the lean times were over, I continued the timing and planning habits. It has become a time management technique for me. I plan my weekly trips to the grocery store and my monthly shopping day well in advance. It enables me to be a smart shopper and avoid over-spending or impulse buying. And when gas prices soar, it's a great fuel-saving habit as well.

Smart Banking

It was somewhere around 1990 when I realized I didn't need a bank. I discovered that a brokerage account offers everything I needed from a bank account with a huge added bonus – I earn interest on every penny. I could make deposits, write checks, transfer funds and get cash with my ATM card. Why did I need a bank account? At first, it seemed too good to be true so I left my bank account open for about a year, waiting for something to happen that would require me to have the bank account after all. But it never happened. Over 20 years later, it still hasn't. I haven't set foot in a bank in all those years for my personal banking needs.

There was only one catch. I had to have a minimum amount of money to open the account. Way back when, it was $10,000, so as soon as I had enough money to open a brokerage account, I did. There was no charge for the account as long as I didn't fall below $1000, and I earned interest every month on every penny. No charge for checks and I could make my deposits by

> *In over 20 years, I haven't set foot in a bank for my personal banking needs.*

mail. The 'Deposit by Mail' envelopes had pre-paid postage so it was easy and free. Never leave your house and do all your banking remotely, earning interest on the entire balance and paying no fees. I even considered it a time management tool because I saved time waiting in line at the bank.

I always thought it was funny that banks charge you money when you bounce a check. You obviously don't HAVE any money or you wouldn't have bounced the check to begin with, so why would they charge you more of what you don't have? George Carlin does a skit on that one too. One of the great things about banking with the brokerage is that if I accidentally write checks for more than I have in the account, they will automatically sweep it from another account. No charge, no fees, no restrictions. Banks can do that too, but there are usually fees and limitations so it gets kind of clumsy.

As for ATM cards, I never withdraw cash at a machine that charges me a fee. Most financial institutions provide complimentary withdrawals as long as you stay within their network. Why pay the fee if I can drive a mile down the road to a machine that doesn't charge a fee?

As a small business entrepreneur, I tried to set up my company banking the same way as my personal banking – at a brokerage. It worked for the main bank account, the one I call the Operations account. But there was a problem with the payroll account. I couldn't find a brokerage institution that allowed for automatic payroll tax payments, so I was forced to open a bank account for my company payroll. But I kept our Operations account at the brokerage. More savings. Interest earned on every penny.

About once a year, I take a look at new brokerage and banking services to see if there's something new I want to use. Financial institutions are always coming up with something new to get your business, so I find it's worth it to check around periodically. Over the years, I've found several gems and I'll happily move my money around to take advantage of them. For example, I found a brokerage that offered a Visa card that paid me back 2% on all my purchases. I found a Visa debit card that has no charges for ATM cash withdrawals – at any ATM in the world!   I found a bank that offered a $100 bonus for opening an account. Recently, I found a credit union that offered a $250 bonus for opening an account. One caution is to always read the fine print. There are often requirements in order to get the deal. For example, the $250 bonus required me to make three deposits, write six online checks, make two transfers and select online statements – all within the first 90 days. If I missed one requirement, I wouldn't get the $250 bonus.

As far as investments, I'm not a financial planner or an investment guru, so I wouldn't dare to advise anyone on how to invest their money. Besides which, when you're digging your way out debt, you don't have any money to invest! But as soon I start having money in my savings account, I start looking for ways to invest it. As an entrepreneur, I tend to want to invest back into my company, but I still like the six month rule I learned as a kid – Always have six months of living expenses ready in case the unexpected happens.

Smart Credit

Now, let's revisit the Czech Payment Plan. You MUST pay your credit card bills in full every month, or you are going to have to pay interest. I'm pretty sure the credit cards know this. In fact, I'm pretty sure they're counting on it! That's why you keep getting invitations to get more credit cards! It's a huge business for them to make money on interest and late fees. The way I see it, they're really making money on my ignorance if I don't pay my bill every month. Let me show you how.

My friend Carol bought a designer purse for $200 on her credit card. But instead of paying it off right away, she proceeded to pay interest on her bill for nearly two years. By the time she paid off her bill, she had paid nearly $350 for that purse, including all the interest charges and fees. Did the purse go up in value? No! So why would she want to pay nearly twice what it's worth? If she pays $350 for the purse over time and the value of the purse is only $200, then she's paying an extra $150 for the instant gratification of having the purse now instead of later – when she can afford it! Sorry Carol, but that's crazy.

Just like my beautiful Scandinavian teak desk, I always wait until I can afford to buy it with cash before I buy it. I have never intentionally paid interest on a credit card. Once, back in my post-divorce days, my Discover card bill was lost in the mail. I never received the statement and I didn't notice it until the next month. When I opened the statement, there was a charge for interest and fees from last month's balance and I was horrified! I think the amount was only $23 but I never forgot it. I cancelled my Discover card too. And that was one thing that was a great help to me when my business got into financial trouble many years later. At least I didn't have credit card debt piled on top of all the other debt.

About Debit Cards

So why bother using a credit card? Why not just use a debit card? If you can't control your spending, then absolutely - use a debit card. Read that again, it's so important. IF YOU CAN'T CONTROL YOUR SPENDING, THEN USE A DEBIT CARD. That's the ONLY reason you should use a debit card.

> *The only reason to use a debit card is if you can't control your spending.*

Using a credit card postpones your payment for up to 30 days. And if I can wait 30 days to pay the bill, then I can earn interest on that money for 30 days – until I write the check. It delays my payment so I get to keep my money a little bit longer before it becomes someone else's money. And I get to earn interest on that money if I have it sitting in an interest-bearing checking account. But that's a very different scenario from charging something that I can't afford, knowing that I'm going to have to pay interest on it. If I charge too much on my credit card and I can't pay it off when the bill arrives, then I'm going to have to pay interest and that defeats the entire purpose.

Debit cards were an ingenious idea for banks and vendors because they get their money right away. But it's not so great for consumers. We give them our money much faster which means we can't earn interest on it. Whoever thought up the idea is probably retired, sipping umbrella drinks on a sandy beach and living off the billions of dollars he or she earned for financial institutions. But it's a lousy idea for the rest of us.

One more note about credit cards

I'm sure credit card companies hate customers like me because they can't make any money off of late payments. I don't feel guilty about it because they make a percentage of every purchase I make in a charge-back to the vendor. That's how credit cards were supposed to work in the first place. But somewhere along the way, they started charging late fees and found it was an even more profitable way to make money, especially for people who run up their credit card bills and just keep paying the interest.

Dave Ramsey suggests that it's better to pay cash and physically touch the money as it leaves you, rather than paying with plastic (debit card or credit card). The logic there is that when you pay with a credit card, you don't see it and feel it going to someone else and that makes it less real. Handing over the cold, hard cash is much more real. Some people have a tendency to spend more if they don't see the cold, hard cash. So be very careful!

Also, keep in mind that if you pay cash for larger ticket items, you can sometimes negotiate for a discount. Vendors like to get cold, hard cash and they're often willing to take less of the green stuff to avoid all the paperwork, hassles and fees of dealing with checks and credit cards.

Smart Car

The two most expensive assets for many people are their car and their house. First, let's talk about cars. Do they appreciate in value? Unless it's a vintage car and you're planning to do something to restore it, the answer is No. According to the Czech Payment Plan, that means I have to pay cash for my car. And that means I may need to take a few steps down in terms of quality and sex appeal. I have to drive a car that matches my means. I've broken this rule a couple of times and I HATED having a car payment.

My dad always said that a car loses 20% of its value when you drive it off the lot and another 20% of its value in the first two years of its existence. So that means I always want to buy a car after it's two years old. Check out car values after the two year mark. They fall off a cliff. Another great lesson from dear old dad. Just be sure you have it checked out by a mechanic before you buy it so you don't get a lemon.

Taking care of your car is important too. And this is where I have to tell my Toyota story. Back in the early 80's, before I got married, I bought a Toyota Corolla. I loved that little car and I was super impressed at everything from the features to the gas mileage. My Corolla was about two and a half years old when someone asked me – "Ellie, how often do you change the oil in your car?" To which I replied, "You're supposed to change the oil?"

I had no idea! The car was running just fine and I assumed all you had to do was put gas in it. I had never pumped up the tires, checked the brakes or checked any of the fluids.

So I took my poor little Toyota Corolla into an auto shop and asked for an oil change. They asked when I had my last oil change and I said Nada. The oil in my car was thick and black, kind of like burnt pea soup, and I'm sure they got a big laugh out of it. But I learned two lessons:

Don't overdo the maintenance. Most manufacturers recommend that you change the oil every 3,000 miles but it's really not necessary. They recommend all kinds of things more frequently than you need them. Why not? It's more money to them when you bring it in for service. That doesn't mean I recommend going two and a half years between oil changes, but if you check the oil periodically, you can see when it's time. My new mechanic says every 6,000 miles is plenty.

Buy Toyota. As much as I love to buy American cars and support American businesses, this is one area where I choose to make an exception. As a single female who knows nothing about cars, the reliability factor is critical to me. I don't want to end up on a deserted road in the middle of nowhere and have my car break down. So for me, it's a safety issue.

After my divorce, it took me four years of driving a Chevrolet Celebrity before I had saved enough money to buy a car outright. I bought a 2 year old Toyota and I've been buying Toyota ever since.

I think it was somewhere in the early 90's when I first heard about car leases. To this day, I think it's one of the biggest rip-offs I've ever heard of. It's like the old health club membership – at the end of the term, what do I have to show for it? Nothing. All I can do is get another lease and start

> At the end of the car loan, you own the car. At the end of the car lease, you own nothing.

paying all over again. Am I building equity? No. In my book, it's like a tax on people who are really bad at math. It's instant gratification for something you can't afford. The low lease payment sounds good in comparison to a loan, but at the end of the loan you own the car. At the end of the lease you own nothing. How smart is that?

Plus it doesn't fit with the Czech Payment Plan so that makes it a non-option for me. I'll never lease, no matter how good the terms look. If I can't pay cash, I can't afford it. And that means I need to lower my expectations to live within my means.

Smart Driving

I used as many smart driving habits as I could. Here's a list of tips and tricks I picked up over the years from various sources:

- Combine all your errands into a single trip and plan out your route to minimize backtracking and wasted miles.

- Carpool if you can. Co-workers, neighbors and friends are all potential participants. Everyone saves money and it's good for the environment.

- Take public transportation. It's generally much cheaper than the cost of gas and maintenance on your car.

- Use human energy by walking or riding a bicycle. Not only will you save gas, you'll get some healthy exercise.

- Live somewhere that enables you to walk to everything.

- Buy nonperishable items in bulk to reduce the number of trips to the store. Warehouse clubs like CostCo and Sam's are great places for bulk purchasing power.

- Work at home. Even if your employer frowns on telecommuting, ask for a compromise of one or two days a week. Every little bit helps.

- Before buying a car, check the fuel mileage estimate. Over the life of the car, it will add up.

- Consider a hybrid car to save on gas, especially if you have a long commute.

- Keep up with basic car maintenance. Check the owner's manual for the manufacturer's recommendation, then adjust it to a level you feel comfortable with.
- Read your owner's manual and always use the manufacturer's recommended grade of motor oil. This can improve your gas mileage by 1 to 2 percent.
- Keep your tires pumped up. Under-inflated tires make the car work harder which burns more gas.
- Lighten your load. Try not to carry extra weight in your car. The lighter your load, the better your gas mileage.

> *Lighten your load. The lighter your load, the better your gas mileage.*

- Turn off the air-conditioner and roll down the windows for some fresh air. You'll improve your gas mileage at the same time. (Note that there has been some heated debate over whether this holds true on the highway where the aerodynamic drag of having your windows down may offset the benefit.)
- Drive the speed limit. The faster you go, the worse your mileage.
- Be sure to use the gasoline recommended by your vehicle's manufacturer. "Stepping up" to a higher octane fuel will not improve your car's performance, but it will cost more money.

- Start and stop gently. Ease onto the gas pedal when starting rather than punching the accelerator. When coming to a stop, ease off the gas pedal in advance and coast a little.

- Shut off the engine. If you have to wait for more than two minutes, it is cost efficient to shut off the engine. Restarting burns less fuel than idling for that long.

- Get the best buy at the pump by filling your gas tank at the coolest times of day--usually early morning or late evening. Gas is denser at these times and gasoline is sold by volume, so you'll actually get more gas for your money!

- Keep your gas tank as full as possible, especially in the summertime. My dad said that the gas evaporates faster in the heat when the gas tank is low. (I've never actually tested or proved this theory, I'm just trusting that he knew more than I did.)

- Don't top off the gas when you're at the pump. It serves no good purpose and you may end up wasting gas if you overflow.

Lastly, check your gas mileage to see how many miles per gallon you're getting. For those who have never calculated miles per gallon in their car, here's how to do it:

1) Fill up the car with gas. Write down the odometer reading. For example, let's assume that the odometer says you're at 20,000 miles.

2) Drive around like you normally would until you've used up at least half a tank.

3) Fill up the car with gas again. Write down the odometer reading and write down the amount of gas you purchased. So, let's say the odometer reading is now 20,300 miles and you purchased 14 gallons.

4) Make the calculation by dividing the number of miles driven (20,300 minus 20,000 = 300 miles driven) by the amount of gas you purchased (14 gallons). In this example, that comes out to 21 miles per gallon.

Recheck your gas mileage periodically. Make note of any changes you've made in your driving habits or car maintenance that are having an effect on the mileage. A steadily declining gas mileage could indicate mechanical problems like a clogged air filter, exhaust system malfunction or deflated tires.

Smart House

Dave Ramsey says you should pay cash for your house. On his popular radio talk show, Dave suggests saving like crazy and living on beans and rice for a few years until you can afford to buy it outright. When you're just starting out and you don't have a plan for anything but survival, that's tough to imagine. But I love the wisdom of it. I think it depends on where you are in your overall financial picture. If you can afford a down payment and you can apply what you would pay in rent to the house payment, then I think it probably makes sense to buy the house. (Remember the Czech payment plan – it must be appreciating in value!)

But look out for sneaky loans. One of the worst, and one that my ex-husband and I argued over, was the balloon payment. The way it works is that you pay interest only on the house for a certain period of years, and then the entire house note comes due. If you're planning to make a million dollars between now and when the loan comes due, then it's a fine idea. You can start living in the house now and you know you'll have enough money to pay the balloon note when it's due. But who knows whether they're going to make a million dollars between now and then? Simply stated: Balloons are bad.

Another sneaky loan is the loan that is tied to the prime interest rate. Those loans are great when the prime mortgage rates are low. Your loan payment is super low too, and that's great. But look out during inflationary times when the interest rates soar thru the ceiling. Your payment will soar up there right along with it. And there is absolutely nothing you can do to change it. You agreed to the terms and you owe the money.

The best type of mortgage is a fixed-rate mortgage. The shorter the term, the less interest you'll be paying over the life of the mortgage loan. The most common options are 15-year and 30-year mortgages. On short term mortgages, the monthly payments will be higher, but you'll pay the loan off much faster (15 years versus 30 years) so you're paying significantly less money over the long haul.

> *The shorter the term, the less interest you'll be paying over the life of the mortgage loan.*

If you're overwhelmed by all the financial terms and options, find a friend or family member who is willing to sit down and explain it to you. Read a book. Research it on the internet. Educate yourself! The easiest prey for scams and greedy salespeople is an uneducated buyer. So do your homework. Don't let the sucker be you!

Smart Entertainment

Enjoyment and laughter are vital aspects of a happy, healthy, balanced life. Therefore, entertainment is worth seeking out, and it comes in lots of different shapes and sizes. There are many forms of entertainment if you're willing to get creative. With a little bit of time, patience and creativity, there are plenty of ways to get entertainment for yourself, your family and your friends that don't cost a penny (or are dirt cheap). Here are some ideas to get you started.

- Card games – There must be a million games you can play with a deck of cards. If you're alone, you can play solitaire games. If you're in a group, you can play games like rummy, hearts, spades, bridge, pinochle, canasta, etc. Buy a book of card games or look online for more ideas.

- Charades – The game of charades requires no monetary investment and you can play it for hours. There are a host of similar games that work the same way.

- Board games – a one-time investment in a board game like Monopoly, Scrabble, Sorry, Clue or Life will reap hours of enjoyment for years to come.

- Activity games – Get outside and play ping-pong, croquette, badminton or horseshoes. Once you've purchased the initial equipment, it doesn't cost any money. You'll get some fresh air and a bit of exercise at the same time.

- Solo games – there are books of puzzle games for the individual – crossword puzzles, sudoku puzzles, logic games, word games, word scramble games, etc. Many puzzles are available free on the internet.

- Get some outdoor exercise. Go for a walk or ride a bike. Try out new routes to change the scenery and keep it interesting. Go for a hike or go bird-watching.

- Read a book. For a family connection, read a book together. One person reads aloud while the others listen. You can talk about each chapter as you finish it for added impact. Kids love it, and your choice of books can have a profound impact on their thinking as they grow up. I'll always remember my mom reading Little Women to my sister and me, and the laughter and the tears as we heard the story unfold. I looked forward to those evening reading sessions with great excitement.

- Go to the library – by yourself or as a family. At the library, each person can explore books that are particularly interesting to him or her.

> Learn a new language, learn how to play a musical instrument, find a new hobby like stamp collecting or fly fishing.

- Learn something new. Learn a new language, learn how to play a musical instrument, find a new hobby like stamp collecting or fly fishing. Read everything you can find about it and give it a try. Have fun with it!

- Create something – do you like to draw, paint, write, sculpture? Here's your chance! Start creating things, in fact, you can create some really cool things from junk. Create colorful murals from bottle caps, handbags from fabric scraps, origami figures from waste paper. If you're creative enough, you may even be able to turn your artistic "junk" into saleable products.

- People watching – go to the mall, the park, the airport, and watch the people go by. For added fun, go with a friend and invent interesting stories about the people going by. "I think that lady grew up in Boston but she hated cold weather so she moved south as soon as she turned 18. She's been working as a secretary ever since and she makes a great apple pie."

- Volunteer – volunteer your time to an animal shelter, a soup kitchen, a hospital or a church. Build a Habitat for Humanity house. Find a way to give back with your time. Not only will you be helping someone else, you'll feel good about yourself and you're likely to make new friends in the process.

- Snouse Hooping – my friend David and I love to wander thru houses that are under construction. We imagine which rooms are which and how they will be decorated by the owner someday. (It's really house snooping but we renamed it "snouse hooping".)

- Gardening – get outside and work in the garden. Pull weeds and rip out all the dead foliage. Plant seeds and nurture them. Dig your hands into the dirt and get your fingernails filthy dirty! If you don't have a yard, use flower pots or old coffee cans and plant things indoors or on a balcony. It's fun to see things grow.

- Collecting – become a collector of something – stamps, coins, thimbles, postcards, baseball cards, buttons, butterflies, etc. Find something that you're interested in and start your collection.

- Scrapbooking – it doesn't have to cost a fortune. Just gather together your mementos and photographs and organize them chronologically and/or topically. Start compiling them in shoe-boxes for organization, then move them into notebooks when you have the time and money.

With creativity and determination, the list can go on and on. The point is that we don't have to spend a fortune on movies, concerts, theme parks, cable TV, sporting events and expensive hobbies. There are plenty of simple options that are already available!

Other Smart Stuff

There were lots of other frugal habits that I followed after my divorce, many of them founded in the Depression Era, I'm sure. I tweaked them to fit my life and my lifestyle. Here are some of the easiest and most common ones I used:

- Instead of eye make-up remover, use baby shampoo or a cocktail of baby oil and water. A tiny bottle of eye make-up remover costs around $5. A big bottle of baby shampoo (5 times as much) can cost half the price. Savings – $22.50.

> Instead of eye make-up remover, use baby shampoo or baby oil and water.

- Don't throw away hosiery that has runs in them. They can function sort of like a wind-directional sock (like you see at small airports). Use them to filter lint on the drain hose of the washing machine or to catch lint on the end of the clothes dryer vent hose. Check them frequently for mold, shake them out and wash them periodically to avoid getting lint everywhere. You can even use old hosiery on plants that need to be staked in the garden, or as stuffing for pillows or craft projects.

- Don't throw away letter-size paper that is only printed on one side. Flip it over, put it in the printer and print on the back side. Free paper!

- Buy movies instead of renting them or going to the movie theater. When you buy it, you get to watch it over and over again for free. Consider renting the movie from the public library first to be sure you like it before you buy it. Otherwise, you just wasted your money.

- If you must go to the movie theater, watch for coupons or specials and go to the afternoon matinees that are usually cheaper. And don't buy their concessions! I always carry a large purse or a backpack when I go to the movies and I bring in my own popcorn and soda. After the lights go down, I enjoy my treats at a fraction of the cost I would have paid in the lobby.

- Instead of eating out, get a To Go box at a buffet and fill it up. As long as they don't charge by weight, I stuff the box until it is overflowing. Sometimes, I can get 3 or 4 meals out of a single box.

- Don't buy expensive make-up at the department store. Walgreens and Walmart have a wide variety of good quality, reasonably priced lines like Revlon, Neutrogena and Cover Girl. Much of it is the same on the inside – it's only the price on the outside that is radically different.

- Be careful about "rewards" credit cards. Be sure that the rewards are worth the annual fee. I prefer a no-annual-fee cash-back card. And be careful about getting multiple rewards cards – you may not accumulate enough points on any one card to make it worthwhile.

I was always on the lookout for more tips and tricks for saving money. Frugal Czechs may be the first people to do re-cycling and we started it hundreds of years ago. We just didn't know what it was called! I am proud to carry on the tradition.

Don't Worry, Be Happy

Sometimes, when things don't look so great, I ask myself – "What's the worst that could happen?" I guess I could end up penniless and homeless, but I can recover from that, right? I did it before. I'll just start over and work my way back up into solid living again. So why should I worry about it? As Bobby McFerrin crooned in 1988, "Don't worry, be happy."

> "In every life we have some trouble
> When you worry you make it double
> Don't worry, be happy…
> Don't worry don't do it, be happy
> Put a smile on your face
> Don't bring everybody down like this
> Don't worry, it will soon pass
> Whatever it is
> Don't worry, be happy…"

I heard this song for the first time a few days after I signed my divorce papers. I was walking around in a fog and trying to absorb what I had just done. I was scared, broke, lonely and very sad. When you're at the bottom, it can't get any worse. And after my divorce, I was feeling pretty low. Yet I knew I would survive it and so I went about the business of surviving with a passion. I stuck to my smart habits and I started rebuilding my life, and pretty soon, some good things started to happen.

First, my parents and I reconciled. We had to forgive each other and we had to work to rebuild our relationship as adults. But it was well worth the effort and I feel blessed every day to have them in my life.

Second, I had an epiphany. It was one of those life-changing moments – a turning point. I remember I was driving down Interstate-85 in Atlanta, heading downtown to a customer's office. The radio was tuned to NPR, playing classical music. A song came on the radio that I hadn't heard since childhood. You know how that is when you hear a song from the past and it takes you back in time. Suddenly the old feelings sweep over you and you're in touch with a part of you that you forgot was even there.

When I heard the song, I didn't know what the piece was. I knew what key it was in, of course, but I couldn't name the composer or the work of art. The feelings that came flooding in were powerful and the tears started to well up in my eyes. I was so overwhelmed, I had to pull off to the side of the road and I sat there like an idiot in rush hour traffic, weeping for some unknown reason while cars drove by honking at me. Maybe I was crying because the music was so beautiful. Maybe I was crying because I remembered the safety of my childhood, thinking and believing that miracles were possible and dreams really do come true. Maybe I was crying because I realized that my childhood dreams had not come true – and they never would. Maybe that was okay but it was a startling realization nonetheless. My life had been filled with choices – some were good and some were bad. But whatever the choices, I was forced to live with the consequences now and forever more into the future. It all hit me at once.

And then something swept over me like a wave. It was a sense of calm and peace, a feeling that everything was okay. It was kind of like God sat down in the seat beside me and spoke to me. I didn't hear the actual sound of His voice, but I felt the words – like a song in my heart. And God gave me two explicit instructions: "Go back to church" and "Start playing the piano again".

When I heard it, it seemed so obvious. Of course! Those were two great passions of my life as a child and I had turned away from both of them when I was 20 years old. But why? I loved them both. They were like dear old friends and I had abandoned them cold turkey. Why had I ignored them for so long? At the time, it was probably an act of rebellion against my parents more than anything else. But now I was in my mid-30's and I had no axe to grind with my parents anymore. The only person I was hurting was myself.

And so I sat in my car on the side of the highway, soaking in what I had just heard. If God Almighty had bothered to come down to my little car on Interstate 85 in Atlanta, Georgia to tell me what to do, then I'd better pay attention. There have been a number of times in my life when I've asked God to tell me what to do. No, I've begged and pleaded for God to tell me what to do and He never did. It never happened on MY schedule when I wanted it. And now here I was, driving down the interstate, minding my own business, not asking for divine intervention and that's when it happened. It may be the only time it ever happens to me in this lifetime, so I decided I better listen.

I was driving down the interstate, minding my own business, not asking for divine intervention and that's when it happened.

And so I found a church home and I started singing in the choir again – just like when I was a child. It was wonderful and fun and energizing. I made new friends and I started re-building my spiritual life, moving from a position of disbelief to a position of joyous faith. It was a long, slow process. In fact, in many ways I'm still on the journey, but it's been a beautiful journey. At the same time,

I started playing the piano again – seriously. I had dabbled at it over the years, but now I began practicing with a vengeance. I started by re-learning songs from my childhood and I worked my way back up to concert-level performance. I played piano in church and pretty soon I was being asked to play in other places – weddings, banquets, churches, elder-care facilities. What a joy to have a spiritual faith and music back in my life again. It happened in an instant, and yet it happened in slow motion. My rediscovery of faith and music has been a slow and steady re-building, and it's still happening. I don't even know where it's heading yet, but I know that it's a part of me, of who I am at the core. I will never abandon these two old friends again.

And as all of this was going on, my business started to grow. I went from two employees to 25 employees and a boatload of contractors in a matter of two years. We moved to a bigger office and we set up a 401K plan. I wrote a business plan for the first time and I established a management team. I started investing in my own business education. After all, I was a college drop-out, a simple piano player. What business did I have running a multi-million dollar company? Who did I think I was? I joined an organization called Young Entrepreneurs' Organization (YEO) and it gave me more education, expanded my horizons, raised the bar for me professionally and helped me grow personally. I met other entrepreneurs from all over the world and soon I began traveling the world to meet with them.

Things were going well. I was blessed.

4

The Ramen Method

> *"Even if you're on the right track,*
> *you'll get run over*
> *if you just sit there."*

Will Rogers, beloved American actor, comic,
columnist, radio personality

Back to the Future

So I had survived two bouts of being broke – first when my parents disowned me and again after my divorce. I lived frugally, worked hard and both times I managed to recover and rebuild. Then I hopped on the entrepreneurial train and charged down the track of running a small business. I thought my days of financial hardship were over. Things were looking good. Little did I know that there was something worse than being broke and I was about to live it.

Fast forward to 2002. After a wildly successful expansion in my company, things had turned south and now my business was crumbling along with my bank account. I was in debt up to my ears. The sense of failure and fear were overwhelming. I realized how much my sense of identity and self-esteem were wrapped up in my business. It was a terrible feeling. At my core, it was embarrassing too. How could I be so stupid and let things get so bad?

Many of my friends had comfortable, corporate jobs. They'd had them for years and as an entrepreneur, I couldn't imagine what that would be like. A steady paycheck – WOW! Paid benefits and a matching 401K – WOW! I was always too busy trying to be sure my employees got a steady paycheck to worry about myself.

My own payroll history looked like a bad EKG and there were many years when I was the lowest paid employee on the payroll. I never told the employees because I didn't want them to think we were in financial trouble, but it's a reality of owning a small business. You do what you have to do to survive.

And there was always this perception that because I owned the business, I had money. I can understand it because I had the same perception of business owners when I was a young employee working

> And there was always this perception that because I owned the business, I had money.

at their companies. I just assumed that whoever owned the company was rolling in money. It may be true for some, but it's not a given. Many business owners put every penny of their personal savings into their company and have no money left to pay their own bills. It's risky, it's stressful and there are no guarantees that you'll ever be able to sell the business and get your money back.

I've always believed that if I were in a comfortable, corporate job with a steady income, I would be a multi-millionaire many times over by now. All it takes is some responsible, frugal choices and saving a healthy chunk of every paycheck. I watched my friends buy new cars and designer fashions, remodel their houses and go on exotic vacations. I assumed they were socking away loads of money too, but I have come to learn that many of them weren't. They just spent what they had earned. And then some. It reminded me of the tortoise and the hare. I was the tortoise, slowly crawling along on meager pay, but saving religiously as I went. The millionaire next door. At one point, it looked like I was going to win the race, but now I had fallen WAY behind. How was I ever going to get back in the game?

From a business perspective, it seemed I needed to do the same thing I had done repeatedly with my personal finances –

1) Determine where the business was financially (You are HERE).
2) Spend less than the business was earning.
3) Earn more.

The first step was ugly. The business was half a million dollars in debt and since I was personally in debt too, I had no leverage. It was a terrible position, but it was important to identify the starting point.

Sadly, I had broken the second step by keeping people on the payroll far too long. But it was never too late to get back on track; in fact, it was the only way out. So I had to cut expenses and that required a number of things: I laid off most of the employees, we closed the office and went virtual with the few remaining people, we had a massive office sale to sell everything we possibly could – furniture, cubicles, office supplies, computers, printers, phone system, etc. I scoured our expenses just like I had done personally, cutting off or cutting back on everything we possibly could.

The third step was going to be super difficult. Our customers' budgets were frozen so it was virtually impossible to sell anything to anyone. But I had to try. I cut our rates drastically to get business. I dug up old customer lists and started calling people from the past, trying to find anyone with a project for us. I attended every local association and organization meeting where I thought I might meet potential customers. I was relentless. For two years, it was a daily struggle and I was in constant fear of the creditors knocking at my door. But eventually, the tide started to turn and larger projects started coming in again. The beauty of it now was that our overhead was super low due to all the cutbacks I had made so our profit margins were stronger than ever.

Within four years, I was able to pay off the debt. I remember the day when we finally hit the break-even point. I was sitting alone in my little home office with my faithful cat, Brie, curled up on the chair beside me. I looked at the financial statements on my screen and decided I needed to see it in print to be sure it was real. So I printed a copy and held it in my hands. It was real. Looking at those statements, it felt like a death sentence had been lifted. First I started laughing with joy and then my eyes welled up with tears. I was overwhelmed at how hard it had been and how fortunate I was that the company had survived. They were tears of joy, relief and exhaustion. I felt like I could exhale for the first time in almost five years.

The Ramen Method Chart

When I talk with people who are in financial distress, I invariably find myself referring back to the same three-step process that I followed. I call it the Ramen Method because I use the visual image of a Ramen noodle to show a person's financial path through life. No matter where you are or where you've been, you can start the three step process and start moving in the right direction.

First, let's look at the Ramen Method chart to learn the basic layout of the chart.

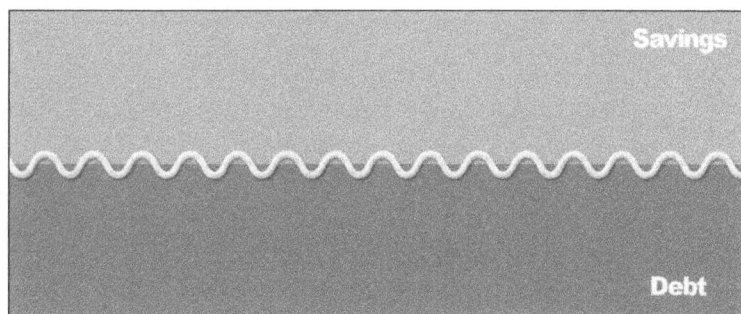

Note the following points:
- Think of the left side of the chart as birth and the right side of the chart as death. The years of your life are stretched across the chart from left to right.
- When the noodle is in the upper part of the chart, you have money. We'll call this part of the chart the SAVINGS area. Anytime you're in the SAVINGS area

of the chart, you have more money than your debts. There are two ways to be in this position.

- o You have money in the bank and you have no debts. This is the strongest possible position to be in financially.

- o You have enough money that you could pay off all of your debts in full and still have money left over. This is also a good position to be in because it means you're not at risk of being unable to pay a debt.

- When the noodle is in the lower part of the chart, you are in debt. That means you owe more money than you have. We'll call this part of the chart the DEBT area. This is not a good position to be in. At any point in time, the people (or banks/financial institutions) that you owe money to, could demand payment from you. And if you can't make the demanded payment, they could take away your property and/or your cash. In cases that go to court, they could even stake a claim against your future earnings (called a Garnishment). Being in the DEBT area is risky.

Next, we'll look at a series of "stories" using this simple structure to illustrate a person's financial position.

Paycheck to Paycheck

The first three stories illustrate living paycheck to paycheck.

Paycheck to Paycheck, Story #1

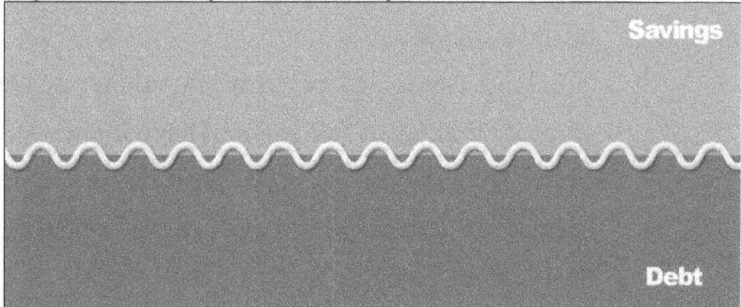

Interpretation – Story #1
This person is living paycheck to paycheck. When they get paid, they have money, but then they spend everything they have and more, going a little into debt. They bounce back and forth between having money and having debt during each pay cycle and they don't make any progress on improving their financial position.

While this person is not in a terrible position, they are still at risk. If they were to become ill, lose their job or face another unexpected catastrophe, they would lose their ability to pay their bills. They have no cushion and they're not doing anything to build one.

Paycheck to Paycheck, Story #2

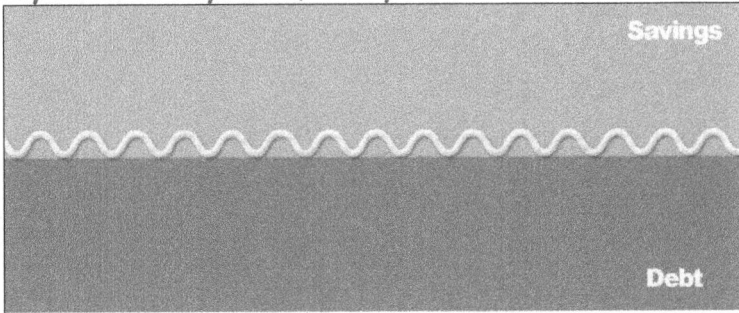

Interpretation – Story #2

This person is also living paycheck to paycheck. When they get paid, they have money, but then they spend every penny they have. Unlike Story #1, this person is careful not to go into debt, but they aren't making any progress on improving their financial position. They are a bit more financially responsible than the person in Story #1 and their credit rating is stronger than the person in Story #1. But they're still at risk of job loss, illness or a catastrophic event.

Paycheck to Paycheck, Story #3

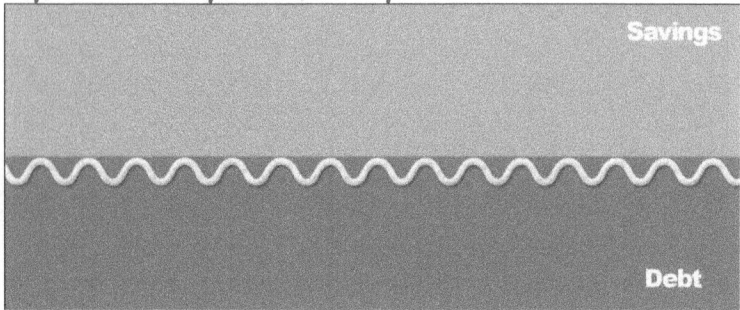

Interpretation – Story #3
This person is living paycheck to paycheck. When they get paid, they have no money, and they continue to spend themselves into debt. Each pay period, they manage to pull themselves up to the baseline and break even, but they aren't making any progress on improving their financial position. They're barely able to pay their bills and they are stuck in the DEBT area. This person is at high risk. Their credit score is probably weak and they could easily slide further into debt if faced with hardship.

Paycheck to Paycheck – Summary

All of the people in these stories are spending exactly what they earn in each paycheck. They may have a false sense of security because they're able to pay their bills each month and their debt isn't increasing. The risk is that their financial position could change drastically if they lost their source of income. They have no emergency commission, no savings. It's kind of like coasting in a car. You're fine until you have to go uphill. Then you need some fuel.

Note that this model could also apply to people who are living on Social Security income, unemployment or other government subsidies.

The Ramen Method: 3–Step Stories

The Ramen Method consists of three steps. The first step is to determine where you are financially right now, today. It's an honest look at the cold, hard truth, good or bad, and it gives you a starting point for moving into steps 2 and 3.

Step #1: You are HERE

This is your current financial position. Are you in debt or do you have money (negative or positive financial net worth)? Exactly how much money and debt do you have? Make a list of what you own and a list of what you owe. Subtract what you owe from what you own. If the result is a positive number, congratulations! You're above the line. If the result is a negative number, you are in debt. You're below the line. For further guidance on how to figure out your "You are HERE" position, refer to Section 2 of this book and read the topic "You Are Here".

Know your starting point. It's the first step to determine where you are financially right now, today. It's an honest look at the cold, hard truth, good or bad, and you'll be referring back to it for comparison as you move forward through Steps 2 and 3.

Step #2: Spend Less than you Earn

No matter where you are right now, if you want to improve your financial position, you must spend less than you earn. Why? Because if you spend more than you earn, you'll go further into debt.

This step requires a detailed study of how you're spending your money. Refer to Section 1 of this book and read the topic "Create a Budget". You'll need to find ways to reduce and/or eliminate expenses enough that your income can pay all the expenses. There are lots of ideas and tips throughout this book to help you do that.

Then, what do you do with the extra money? First you save it until you have your emergency cushion. Three to six months of living expenses should give you a good cushion. (Don't touch the cushion unless you have a true emergency!) Then, if you still have debt, you use the extra money to pay it off. And after the debt it paid off, you save the extra money.

Step #3: Earn More
No matter how much you earn today, one sure-fire way to increase your financial picture is to earn even more money. This gives you another cushion that enables you to save more money.

There are several ways to earn more money. You could ask for a job promotion, take on a 2nd job, get contract work or take on odd jobs. You could create an internet storefront and sell something. You could flip houses or invest in real estate and become a landlord. You could dabble in entrepreneurship and start your own small business. (Many large businesses today started out as an entrepreneurial experiment in someone's basement.) Having multiple sources of revenue is a protection for you in the event that one source of revenue goes away. I call it "revenue diversification" and I'm more convinced than ever that it is an important trend in personal financial stability.

(After my third bout with financial distress, I decided to create multiple income streams to achieve revenue diversification. I started two new businesses, recorded a CD of piano music, started public speaking and invested in a few other start-up businesses. I believe this strategy is the main reason why I weathered the latest economic downturn so well. And it gives me hope that I won't get into financial trouble again.)

Job security in today's financial environment is fleeting. The days of long-tenured employment and retirement with a gold watch are gone. The result is that the loyalty factor between employees and employers is weaker than it was just ten years ago. Revenue diversification gives you both strength in negotiating and options if you lose a source of revenue.

Finally, what do you do with the extra money? Again, if your answer is to spend it, you're perpetuating the behaviors that got you in trouble in the first place. The extra money should be saved. First build the emergency cushion, then pay off your debt, and then invest the rest. Keep saving as much as you can every month.

"You Are HERE" Story

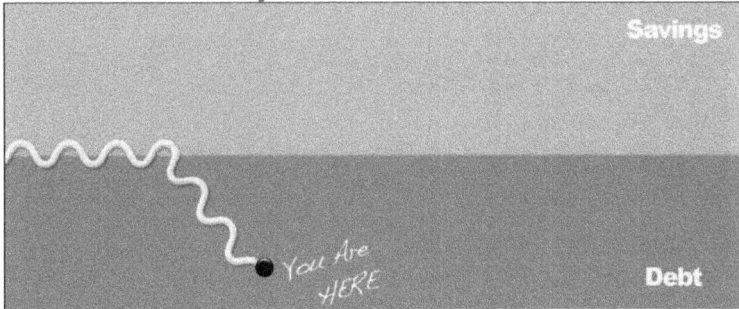

Interpretation – "You are HERE" Story
This person started out living paycheck to paycheck, but then they started spending more than they earned every pay period. This steadily moved them down into the Debt area. Now, this person has choices on how to move forward financially. If they continue to spend more money than they earn, as they have been doing recently, they will continue to go further into debt. However, if they move into Steps 2 and 3 of the Ramen Method, they can change their direction upward instead of downward and change their future.

Financial Recovery Story

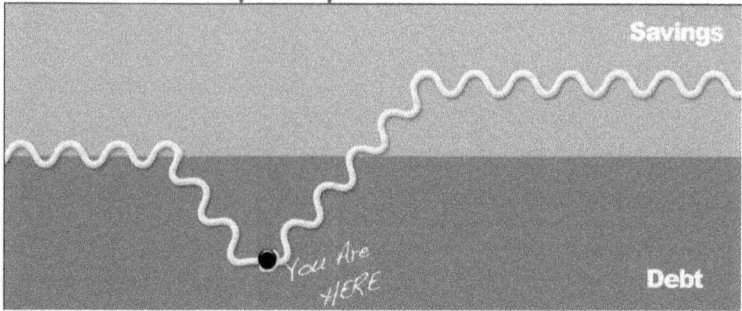

Interpretation – Financial Recovery Story
Continuing from the previous chart, this person started out in debt (You Are HERE).   Then they made changes in their spending and earning habits that enabled them to earn more than they were spending. This enabled them to pay off their debt and start accumulating more money. According to the chart, they have continued their smart money management skills and stayed "in the money". And they all lived happily ever after...

Not-So-Successful Stories

These stories illustrate scenarios that were not successful. Unfortunately, these people didn't use the Ramen Method!

Silver Spoon Story

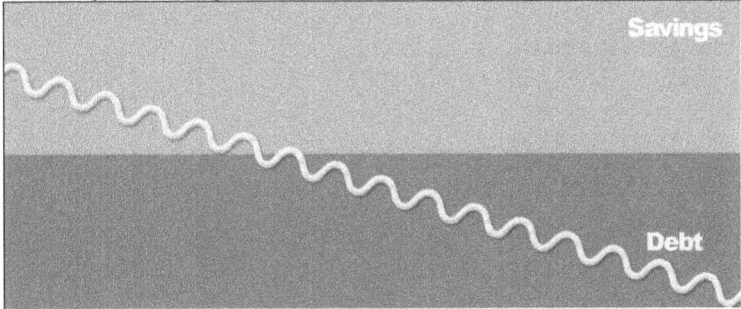

Interpretation – Silver Spoon Story
This person started their life with a lot of money, the proverbial silver spoon. Perhaps they were born into a wealthy family or perhaps they received a large inheritance at an early age.

Unfortunately, this person never learned good money management skills. Throughout their life, they spent more money than they earned, so they steadily spent all of their savings and proceeded to go deeply into debt.

Bankruptcy Story, Part 1

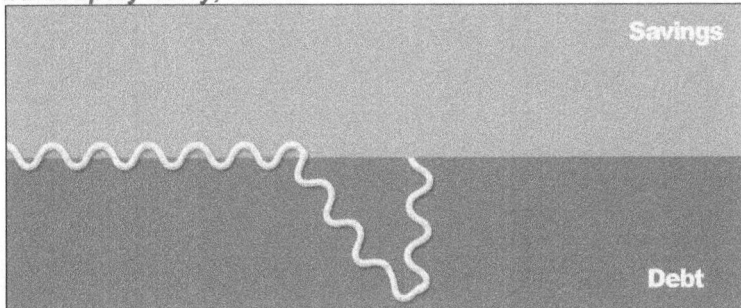

Interpretation – Bankruptcy Story, Part 1
This person started out living paycheck to paycheck. At some point, they started spending more than they earned, and this drove them deeply into debt.

The person filed for bankruptcy, a legal process that removes a person's debt. This is the point where they move back up to the baseline. The slate is clean and they can choose how they will manage their money in the future.

Bankruptcy Story, Part 2

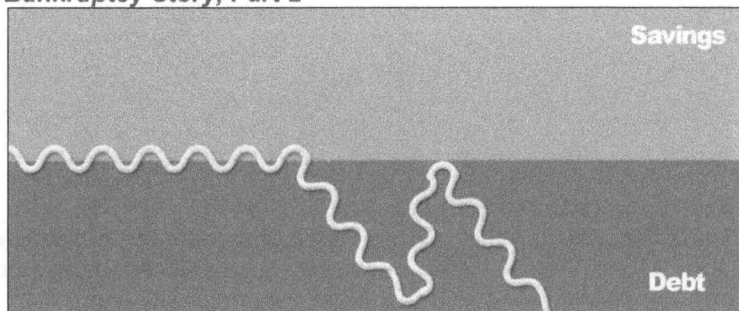

Interpretation – Bankruptcy Story, Part 2
Sadly, this person returned to their lifelong behavior of spending more than they earned. This drove them straight back into debt. A startling number of people who claim bankruptcy go right back into debt because they haven't changed their financial behaviors.

Successful Stories

These stories illustrate scenarios where people successfully managed their money and got out of debt.

Entrepreneur Story

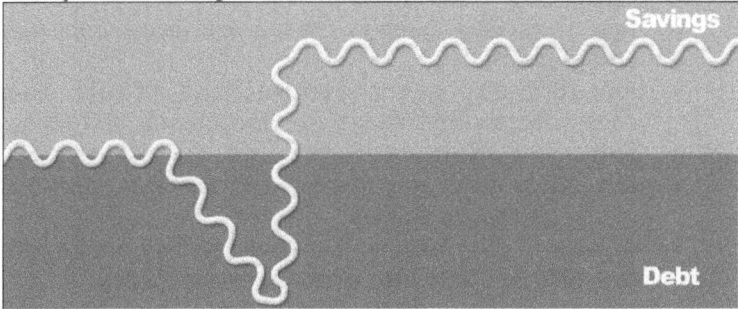

Interpretation – Entrepreneur Story
This person started out living paycheck to paycheck. Then, they decided to take a risk at entrepreneurship and start a company. Although we can't tell whether this was a calculated risk, we can see the entrepreneur move further and further into debt as they are building their company. Then we see a sharp upward movement from Debt into Money when they successfully sold their business. Thankfully, this person continued to manage their money wisely and live a financially comfortable lifestyle into the future.

Life Story

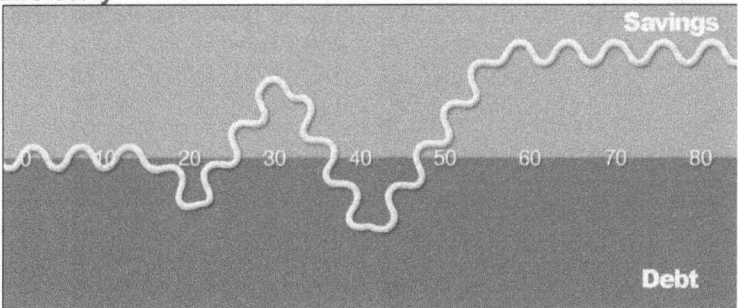

Interpretation – Life Story
This chart illustrates someone's financial life from start to finish. You can see the person's age advancing in 10 year increments across the chart. Here's the scenario:

- Age 0 to 17 – at the baseline
- Age 17 to 26 – goes to college and incurs debt from college loans
- Age 26 to 35 – gets a great job, pays off debt, starts saving money and moves comfortably into the Money area
- Age 35 to 45 – gets married and has kids, spending more than they're earning
- Age 45 to 65 – gets serious about getting out of debt, spending less than they earn and saving money
- Age 65 to 80 – retires with sufficient savings to live comfortably

Each of these stories offers a window into financial behaviors and how they affect a person's financial position.

It's all about having a plan. Sometimes I think having a plan can be as important as the plan itself. If there's no plan at all, life just happens. It applies to many aspects of life – health, career, relationships and more. I don't want my life to just happen to me. I prefer to have more control than that, financially and otherwise. So I'm diligent about setting goals and developing plans on how to achieve them.

Economics and Fads

There have been economic downturns throughout history. In the United States, the first significant downturn occurred in 1797 and more significant downturns have popped up regularly ever since – about once every 10 to 15 years on average. Money management skills become increasingly important during economic downturns as people try to navigate through job loss, inflation, deflation and other financial landmines.

As an individual, I don't believe I can affect the economic downturn or recovery of the United States of America. I can eliminate the Starbucks on the way to work every morning. I can bring in a brown bag lunch to avoid eating out. I can review my finances regularly to be sure I'm on track. But I can't fix the global economy. I can't stop global warming. I can try my best to help in small ways. I can do the next right thing. But beyond that, I simply can't worry about it. It is what it is.

> I can't fix the global economy or stop global warming. But I can try my best to help and I can do the next right thing.

There are two fads that entered the market in the past decade in a big way. One is organic food and the other is the "green" movement. I believe that both of them are rooted in wisdom to serve a good cause. But

I'm also mildly suspicious of how these movements have become commercialized. Are we really making a difference by paying up to twice the normal cost for these products, or are we falling prey to good marketing and branding campaigns. It feels a bit like the designer brands and celebrity brands. Is there really a difference in the products?

How much of the fads are real? I recently heard that tap water is just as healthy as bottled water anyway. How much more money would I have today if I could recover what I've spent on bottled water in the past 10 years?

And sometimes the two fads are in conflict. Who could say how many billions of plastic water bottles have been used to give us healthier water and how many landfills are overflowing with empty water bottles?

In tough economic times, when I'm using empty butter tubs and Cool Whip containers to avoid buying new Tupperware, can I really afford to spend double the cost on a head of organic lettuce? Who knows where those organic vegetables were really grown? They look identical. Are those carrots really any different? And even if they are, can I afford to pay double?

Yes, I want to eat healthy and I want to help save our planet. But I'm going to research fluorescent light bulbs before I rush out to the store and buy them. I want to feel confident that the fluorescent bulbs will save energy, lower my power bill and emit a fraction of the heat produced by incandescent bulbs. In the case of florescent bulbs, based on my research, they do what they say and last so much longer that they really ARE a smart buy, so I'm in. But I'm cautious about all of these fads. I'm not going to rush to the store to buy the next fad product. In my mind, it's just being smart.

To me, being smart means living frugally all the time. Even though I'm on solid financial footing today, I still shop at CostCo and Walmart and SteinMart – all discount stores. Why pay more? I watch for special sales and I use coupons when I can. I order online to save time and even more money. And I still eat Ramen noodles for dinner sometimes. Who can beat dinner for 17 cents? Thankfully, I eat Ramen noodles because I actually LIKE them. It gives me warm, fuzzy memories of the tough times and it makes me thankful that I'm eating them now because I want to, not because I have to.

Knowing this, the smartest thing I can do is focus on what I can control. And that means I should be following good money management skills, namely the Ramen Method, in good times and bad times. If I stick with that, I'll be better prepared to weather the storm when it arrives. And as life has taught me, the storms will arrive.

So no matter where I am in life, financially or otherwise, I can still be frugal. It keeps me humble and it's just plain smart.

Recalculating

When I make a wrong turn on the road, my reliable GPS lady politely says "Recalculating". Sometimes, when I'm really lost, I'll make several wrong turns in a row, trying to get back on track. She keeps saying "Recalculating. Recalculating. Recalculating."

It occurs to me that life is much the same way. I thought I was going to grow up and be a concert pianist. I would get married, have a boatload of kids and live in a house with a white picket fence. There would be a big dog in the back yard and two cats in the house. We would have friends over for dinner and our parties would be the talk of the town. Twice a year, I would travel the world to play piano concerts and the rest of the time I would teach piano lessons to neighborhood kids. On our 20th anniversary, my husband (the best doctor in town) and I would repeat our wedding vows and we would be even more in love than on the day we met. That was the road I thought I was headed down. But that's not what happened.

I got disowned. Recalculating. I got divorced. Recalculating. I nearly went bankrupt. Recalculating. Suffice it to say, life is a series of adjustments and recalculations. Maybe the people who are most successful in life are the ones who are the most adept at recalculating. Change is inevitable and continuous. I know that I will have plenty more opportunities to recalculate in my life. But I'm actually looking forward to it now. I embrace the possibilities!

When I was in the first grade, we read a little book called "Room Enough". It must be out of print now because I can't find it, but I still remember it. It was about a couple that lived on a farm. They complained to a wise old man that their house wasn't big enough. They didn't have enough room to live a normal life. The wise old man advised them to bring their goat into the house to live with them. And so they did, but it didn't help. They went back to the wise old man and complained again. He advised them to bring their horse into the house too. And so they did, but that didn't help either. They returned to the old man again. Each time, he advised them to bring more animals into the house, until eventually, the house was so full, they couldn't move! Then, finally, the wise old man told them to take all the animals out of the house. And suddenly, their house seemed huge! Now, at last, they had "room enough".

The process of bringing each of the animals into the house, and eventually, moving all of them back out of the house is similar to how I felt as I was stopping the bleeding after near bankruptcy, and slowly recovering afterwards. As I continued to recover, I began turning things on again, restarting the old habits. I turned the heat back on in winter and the A/C in summer. The cleaning lady came back and the lawn doctor started sprinkling magic dust on my grass again. I re-started the decadent semi-annual teeth cleaning and I let myself eat out once in a while.

Even so, I view those things differently now. I don't take them for granted. And I don't need them. For me, it's important that I recognize that. Yes, I may be in a position to choose whether I'm willing to spend money on those things, but I'm also aware that it can all be gone in an instant. I don't have to live like a pauper but I don't have to be extravagant either. There's a balance, somewhere in the middle. We each have to find our own middle, and I imagine the middle changes for each of us as we go through life.

> I don't have to live like a pauper and I don't have to be extravagant. There's a balance, somewhere in the middle.

God help me, I'd better never have a house that's bigger than Warren Buffet's. And I can't imagine why anybody would. That's why I still drive a car that's 10 years old and I'll happily drive it into the ground. That's why I'll never remodel a perfectly good, functional kitchen to match the latest trends on HGTV. That's why I won't buy a new washer or dryer before my old one breaks down. If I have enough money to do those things, that's nice to know. But how much better to help a starving child in

Africa, or contribute to cancer research, or do a million and one other things that matter more than new granite countertops.

I didn't used to think that way, and I guess that's part of a recalculation I'm going through right now. When I almost lost my business, I felt like a failure as a business owner and as a person. But they aren't one and the same. I'm the same person whether I'm riding high or half a million dollars in debt. My family and my real friends are there for me either way.

There have been many events in my life that have caused me to recalculate, and there will be plenty more I'm sure. Each time, I learn a little more, I grow a little more and I gain a new perspective. I can eat Ramen noodles seven days a week if I have to and I wouldn't even be surprised if it happened to me again. I'm not afraid of that anymore. Life is full of surprises and who knows what tomorrow holds? For now, it's nice to know I can splurge, every once in a while. It's even nicer to know that I don't need to splurge to be a happy, whole person. That's a blessing, all by itself.

5

Ramen Noodle Recipes

> *"Once during prohibition,*
> *I was forced to live for days*
> *on nothing but food and water."*

W.C. Fields, an American comedian, actor
juggler and writer, known for his comic persona
as a hard-drinking egotist and sympathetic character

3 Bean Ramen Salad

Serves: 2

Ingredients:

1 (3 oz) package any flavor ramen noodles
1/2 cup green beans
1/2 cup kidney beans
1/2 cup lima beans
1/4 cup Italian dressing

Directions:

1. Cook noodles according to package directions and drain.

2. Add beans and sprinkle on dressing.

7 Layer Chinese Salad

Serves: 2-3

Ingredients:

1 (3 oz) package oriental flavored ramen noodle soup mix
5 cups torn romaine lettuce
2 cups diced cooked chicken
10 oz pkg. frozen corn, thawed and drained
1 tomato, diced
2 green onions, thinly sliced
1/2 cup chopped peanuts
2 Tbsp sugar
1/2 tsp salt
1 tsp grated ginger root
1/4 tsp pepper
1/4 cup oil
3 Tbsp apple cider vinegar

Directions:

1. Place romaine in bottom of large serving bowl.

2. Crush the ramen noodle and save the seasoning packet for another recipe.

3. Sprinkle noodles, chicken, corn, tomato, green onions, and peanuts over lettuce in bowl.

4. In a small bowl, combine sugar, salt, ginger root, pepper, oil, and vinegar and stir with wire whisk until well blended.

5. Pour over salad in bowl and serve.

Antipasto Ramen Salad

Serves: 1-2

Ingredients:

1 (3 oz) package any flavor ramen noodles
1/4 cup pepperoni, sliced
1/4 cup black olives
1/8 cup bermuda onion, sliced
Italian dressing

Directions:

1. Cook noodles according to package directions and drain.

2. Add pepperoni, olives and onions.

3. Sprinkle on dressing and toss.

Crockpot Beef and Noodles

Serves: 4-6

Ingredients:

2-3 lb cooked roast beef
6 (3 oz) packages any flavor ramen noodles
2 cups water

Directions:

1. Cook 2 to 3 lb beef roast in the Crockpot with around a cup of water on low overnight.

2. In morning shred meat and add 6 packages of ramen noodle seasoning.

3. Add additional 1/2 cup of water

4. Cook remainder of the day

5. 1 hr before serving add 6 packages of ramen noodle bricks to Crockpot.

6. Add additional 1/2 cup of water

Crunchy Cabbage Salad

Serves: 2-4

Ingredients:

2 (3 oz) packages any flavor ramen noodles
1/4 cup sesame seeds
1/3 cup sliced almonds
1 head cabbage, shredded
1 red bell pepper, sliced
1 orange bell pepper, sliced
1 cup snow peas
6 green onions, thinly sliced
1/2 cup oil
1/4 cup apple cider vinegar
2 Tbsp sugar
1/4 tsp pepper

Directions:

1. Toast sesame seeds and almonds in microwave on high for 2-3 minutes, stirring frequently.

2. In a large bowl, combine cabbage, peppers, snow peas, and green onions.

3. In a medium bowl, combine oil, water, vinegar, sugar, and 1 seasoning packet.

4. Beat dressing with wire whisk until combined.

5. Crush ramen noodles and save the seasoning packet for another recipe.

6. Just before serving, toss crushed noodles, toasted almonds and sesame seeds with cabbage mixture.

7. Pour dressing over salad and toss well.

Doritos Ramen Salad

Serves: 2-3

Ingredients:

2 (3 oz) packages beef flavored ramen noodles
1 (10 oz) bag Doritos
1 lb ground beef
2 cups shredded cheddar cheese

Directions:

1. Cook ramen noodles according to package directions (only use 1 of the seasoning packets) and drain.

2. Cook ground beef adding 1 of the seasoning packets to the beef mixture.

3. Mix beef and ramen noodles.

4. On a plate, place Doritos to make a "bed" for the beef mixture.

5. Place beef mixture on top of Doritos and top with cheddar cheese.

Dr. Dave's Ramen Casserole

Serves: 1-2

Ingredients:

1 (3 oz) package of beef or chicken flavored ramen noodles
Crushed red pepper (to taste)
Chili powder (to taste)
Tabasco sauce (to taste)
Sriracha hot chili sauce (to taste)
1 package of frozen mixed vegetables (stir-fry, Italian, oriental, or your
    choice)
1 1/2 cup water

Directions:

1. Put 1 package of ramen noodles in the bottom of a casserole dish.
    Sprinkle the seasoning packet over the top.

2. Add spices to taste – crushed red pepper, chili powder, Tabasco
    sauce or Sriracha hot chili sauce

3. Add 1 package of frozen mixed vegetables over the top.

4. Pour 1 1/2 cups of water over the top.

5. Cook in microwave for 5 minutes, stir and microwave for 3 more
    minutes.

Egg Drop Ramen

Serves: 1

Ingredients:

1 (3 oz) package chicken flavored ramen noodles
1 egg
soy sauce
chives (optional)

Directions:

1. Follow the directions for ramen noodles on package.

2. Bring water to a boil, add noodles and turn down heat.

3. Beat an egg with a fork in a separate bowl. As the noodles are cooking, slowly pour the egg into the mix and stir.

4. When noodles are done cooking add seasoning packet, soy sauce to your tastes and garnish with chives.

Layered Ramen Casserole

Serves: 2-3

Ingredients:

2 (3 oz) packages chicken flavored ramen noodles
1 lb ground beef
3 eggs
2 cups shredded cheese (any kind)
1 Tbsp minced onion (rehydrated)
1 cup spaghetti sauce

Directions:

1. Preheat oven to 325 degrees.
2. Separate the ramen noodles from their flavor packets.
3. Brown meat, mixing in 1 ramen noodle flavor packet and the rehydrated onion (add the other ramen flavor packet if beef needs more flavor) and drain.
4. Pour meat into the bottom of 8x8 dish or 2qt glass dish (both work).
5. Sprinkle 1/2 cup cheese over the top of beef while it's still hot.
6. Cook egg to your preference in same pan as beef.
7. Place egg on top of beef and add another 1/2 cup cheese.
8. Boil ramen noodles until softened and drain.
9. Mix spaghetti sauce into ramen noodles and pour on top of the eggs.
10. Sprinkle the rest of the cheese on top of the noodles.
11. Place in oven for 10 minutes or until cheese is melted.

Quiche of Ramen

Serves: 4-6

Ingredients:

1 (3 oz) package any flavor ramen noodles, crushed
1 (10 oz) package frozen spinach, chopped, defrosted, drained and
    squeezed
3 oz chicken breasts, cooked, chopped 1/4 inch
1/2 cup red pepper, thinly sliced
1 medium onion, chopped
1 (10 fluid oz) can sliced mushrooms, drained (optional)
1 stalk celery, chopped (optional)
2 garlic cloves, smashed
salt and pepper
6 eggs, beaten
2/3 cup milk
2 tsp sambal oelek
1 tsp oregano
1/4 cup parmesan cheese, grated (optional)

Directions:

1. Preheat oven to 375°F.

2. Lightly grease a 9" deep pie plate or quiche dish.

3. Break uncooked ramen noodles apart and spread evenly in the
    bottom of the pie plate.

4. Cover the noodles evenly with the well drained, squeezed spinach

5. Add the cooked, diced chicken, onion, and red pepper.

6. Add the drained mushrooms and celery (if using).

7. Season with salt and pepper to your taste.

8. Beat the eggs and milk together.

9. Add the sambal olek, garlic and oregano to the eggs and mix.

10. Pour eggs over the vegetables.

Quiche of Ramen, cont.

11. Bake at 375F for 45 min.

12. After 30 min add the parmesan cheese on top and return to oven for approximately 15 minutes to finish cooking.

Quick Ramen Frittata

Serves: 2-4

Ingredients:

2 (3 oz) pkgs. chicken flavored ramen noodles
6 eggs
1 Tbsp. butter
1/2 cup shredded Cheddar cheese

Directions:

1. Place noodles in a saucepan filled with boiling water.

2. Cook noodles until tender and drain.

3. In a medium bowl, whisk together the eggs and 1 of the seasoning packets from the noodles. Save the remaining seasoning packet for another recipe.

4. Add cooked, drained noodles to egg mixture.

5. Melt butter in a large skillet over medium heat.

6. Add the egg/noodle mixture and cook over medium-low heat until firm, 5 to 7 minutes..

7. Cut frittata into four wedges, and turn over to brown the other side for 1 to 2 minutes.

8. Sprinkle cheese over the top, cover pan, and let stand 1-2 minutes.

Ramen Beef Pie

Serves: 2

Ingredients:

2 (3 oz) packages of any flavor ramen noodles
1 lb of ground beef
1 can of sweet corn
1/2 cup of onions
1/3 cup of vegetable oil (cooking)
2 cups of water

Directions:

1. Put 2 cups of water in a cooking pot and bring to a boil.

2. Once the water is boiling add your ramen noodles.

3. Cook 2-3 minutes until the noodles are tender then strain.

4. Heat the vegetable oil and brown ground beef with onions.

5. Pre-heat oven to 350F.

6. Add noodles, ground beef and onions in pot.

7. Add drained sweet corn on top of ground beef and noodles.

8. Cook in the oven for 10-15 minutes.

Ramen Cookies

Yields: 24 cookies

Ingredients:

4 (3 oz) packets ramen noodles
1 (16 oz) bag dark chocolate chips
12-14 drops peppermint extract
1-2 drop spear mint extract
1-2 drop wintergreen extract
24 lollipop sticks or popsicle sticks
1/2 teaspoon butter (optional)

Directions:

1. Crush uncooked ramen noodles in a bowl. Don't crush too finely or the recipe will not set. Set aside.
2. Lay out some wax paper.
3. In a saucepan or double boiler, melt your chocolate chips until they become smooth and creamy.
4. If desired add butter.
5. Slowly add mint extracts to the chocolate and stir for 1 minute.
6. Quickly pour over your crushed ramen noodles and stir vigorously until covered completely.
7. Spoon mixture in tablespoons onto wax paper into round cookie shapes – cookies will flatten considerably so leave a lot of space between them.
8. Place a stick into each cookie before it hardens.
9. Let cool for about an hour.

Ramen Corn Chowder

Serves: 2

Ingredients:

1 (3 oz) package chicken flavored ramen noodles
2 cups water
1 (15 1/4 oz) can whole kernel corn, drained
1 (14 3/4 oz) can cream-style corn
1 cup milk
1 tsp dried onion flakes
1/4 tsp curry powder
3/4 cup shredded cheddar cheese
1 Tbsp minced fresh parsley
1 Tbsp crumbled cooked bacon

Directions:

1. In a small saucepan, bring water to a boil.

2. Break noodles into large pieces and add to saucepan with seasoning packet.

3. Reduce heat to medium and cook uncovered for 2-3 minutes until noodles are tender.

4. Stir in corn, cream style corn, milk, onion, and curry powder and heat thoroughly.

5. Stir in cheese, bacon, and parsley.

Ramen Noodle Alfredo

Serves: 1-2

Ingredients:

1 (3 oz) package any flavor ramen noodles
2 cups water
1/2 cup margarine
1/2 cup light cream
1 cup parmesan cheese, grated
1 Tbsp parsley flakes
1/4 tsp salt
dash of pepper

Directions:

1. Cook noodles as directed on package and drain.

2. Heat butter and cream in a small sauce pan over low heat until margarine is melted.

3. Stir in the rest of the ingredients. Keep warm over low heat until desired thickness is reached.

4. Serve sauce over noodles.

Ramen Noodle Peanut Bread

Serves: 6–8

Ingredients:

1 egg
1 (3 oz) package any flavor ramen noodles
1 1/2 teaspoons nutmeg
1 cup salted peanuts (finely chopped)
1/2 cup low fat cottage cheese
1 cup sugar
2 cups all-purpose flour
1 tsp vanilla extract
1 tsp baking powder
1/2 cup unsalted butter
1/2 cup low-fat milk
1 Tbsp margarine

Directions:

1. Boil two cups of water.

2. Remove from heat, add ramen noodles and let noodles soak for 2 minutes. Do not use the seasoning packet.

3. Strain water from noodles and blot dry with a paper towel.

4. Place noodles on a cutting board and cut until noodles are about 1" long.

5. Preheat oven to 350F.

6. In a bowl use an electric mixer to mix flour, sugar, nutmeg, baking powder, vanilla, egg, milk, and cottage cheese together until well blended.

7. Add ramen noodles and mix well with spoon.

8. Add 1/2 cup chopped peanuts into batter.

9. Grease inside of baking dish with pat of margarine.

Ramen Noodle Peanut Bread, cont.

10. Pour batter into baking dish.

11. Sprinkle remaining peanuts over uncooked batter.

12. Bake for 50-60 minutes or until inserted toothpick in middle comes out clean.

Ramen Noodle Pizza

Serves: 1-2

Ingredients:

1 (3 oz) package any flavor ramen noodles
1 Tbsp olive oil
1 (14 oz) jar spaghetti sauce
1 cup low-fat mozzarella cheese, shredded
3 oz turkey pepperoni
1/2 tsp dried oregano

Directions:

1. Heat oven to broil.
2. Cook ramen noodles according to package directions and drain. Save the seasoning packet for another recipe.
3. Heat olive oil in large skillet.
4. Add noodles to skillet and press down with spatula to cover bottom of pan evenly.
5. Cook 2 minutes or until noodles are browned on bottom.
6. Spread spaghetti sauce over noodles,
7. Add half the pepperoni, all cheese, then remaining pepperoni and oregano.
8. Broil 2 minutes 4-5 inches from heat or until cheese starts to brown.
9. Let cool about 5 minutes before cutting slices.

Ramen Omelet

Serves: 2

Ingredients:

1 (3 oz) package any flavor ramen noodles, broken into small pieces.
2 Tbsp ghee (clarified butter)
4-5 green onions, thinly sliced
1/4 red bell pepper, chopped
1/4 green bell pepper, chopped
1/2 cup cooked chicken, chopped
3 eggs, lightly beaten
salt
fresh ground black pepper
salsa

Directions:

1. Cook ramen noodles as directed on the package and drain. Do not add seasoning packet.
2. While the ramen is cooking, heat an 8 inch sauté pan over medium-high heat.
3. Add Ghee.
4. Saute (stir-fry) onions and bell peppers until onions are translucent.
5. Season egg mixture to taste with salt and pepper.
6. Mix noodles with onions and bell peppers.
7. Add egg mixture, stir and spread evenly over bottom of the pan.
8. Cook until brown, 4-5 minutes.
9. Turn and cook other side the same.
10. Cut into wedges and serve with salsa

Ramen Skillet Supper

Serves: 2

Ingredients:

2 (3 oz) packages oriental or beef flavored ramen noodles
1 lb lean ground beef or ground turkey
2 1/2 cups water
1/2 cup stir-fry sauce
3 cups frozen broccoli carrots cauliflower mix

Directions:

1. Brown meat in large skillet and drain.

2. Add water and 1 of the seasoning packs, stir fry sauce, and frozen veggies.

3. Mix well and bring to a boil.

4. Reduce heat to medium-low cover and cook for 5 minutes or until veggies are tender.

5. Break up the ramen noodles and add to the skillet.

6. Cover and cook 5 to 8 minutes stirring occasionally until sauce is as thick as you like.

Ramen Snack Mix

Serves: 1-2

Ingredients:

1 (3 oz) package any flavor ramen noodles (crushed)
1/2 cup dried cranberries
1/4 cup sliced almonds
1/4 cup dried apricot
1/3 cup of vegetable oil

Directions:

1. While the noodles are still in the package, break them in small pieces.

2. Heat the vegetable oil in the cooking pan.

3. Put your noodles in the cooking pan.

4. Your noodles are ready once they have a nice brownish color.

5. Turn off the stove and put your noodles in a bowl.

6. Add the sliced almonds, dried cranberries and dried apricots.

Ramen Spaghetti

Serves: 1-2

Ingredients:

2 (3 oz) ramen noodle packages
Spaghetti sauce, homemade or one jar of your favorite

Directions:

1. Cook ramen noodles as directed on package but don't add the
    flavor packets.

2. Drain the water and add spaghetti sauce.

3. Then, heat the mixture in the microwave for 1 minute.

4. Serve.

Ramen Taco Bowls

Serves: 1-2

Ingredients:

1 (3 oz) package any flavor ramen noodles
1/2 lb lean hamburger
2 Tbsp finely chopped onions
3/4 cup can diced tomato, drained
2 Tbsp taco seasoning
1 cup water
1/4 cup shredded Mexican blend cheese
1/4 cup crushed tortilla chips
sour cream (garnish)
salsa (garnish)

Directions:

1. Brown meat with onion and drain.

2. Stir in tomatoes, taco seasoning and water. Bring to a boil.

3. Add ramen noodles and save the seasoning package for another recipe.

4. Cook and stir for 3 to 5 minutes or until noodles are tender.

5. Spoon into bowls and sprinkle with cheese and tortilla chips.

6. Serve with sour cream and salsa for additional garnish.

Ramen Tuna Noodle O's

Serves: 1-2

Ingredients:

1 (3 oz) package chicken or creamy chicken flavored ramen noodles
1 1/2 cups water
1 (6 oz) canned tuna
1/3 Tbsp parmesan cheese
1 Tbsp butter
parsley flakes (optional)
black pepper (to taste)

Directions:

1. In deep cereal bowl, add water.

2. Break up the noodles before opening.

3. Add seasoning packet and noodles to water.

4. Microwave Hi 4-5 minutes.

5. Add tuna, parmesan, butter, pepper.

6. Stir well and enjoy.

Spam Supreme Ramen

Serves: 1-2

Ingredients:

1 (3 oz) package any flavor ramen noodles
4 slices Spam
1 clove garlic - lightly smashed
1 egg
1 head/crown broccoli, cut into florets, washed and drained
Peanut Oil

Directions:

1. Cook ramen noodles as directed on the package and add clove of garlic to ramen and boiling water.

2. Shortly after dropping ramen in, drop in broccoli and continue to boil until both are tender.

3. Drain and rinse under cold water.

4. Start boiling water in a kettle.

5. Heat oil on stove and cook egg.

6. When egg whites set add 2 tsp of water and continue to cook.

7. When egg is complete remove and sauté spam in remaining oil.

8. Add boiling water, broccoli, ramen noodles to pan with1/2 package of soup base.

9. Put contents into a serving bowl and top with egg.

Suicide Ramen

Serves: 2-3

Ingredients:

2 (3 oz) packages any flavor ramen noodles
10 packets Taco Bell fire sauce
1 bottle Tabasco
1 Finely chopped habanera pepper
 cheese, grated (your choice)

Directions:

1. Cook ramen noodles as directed on package.

2. As ramen cooks, add Taco Bell fire sauce, Tabasco and habanera
    pepper.

3. When finished, put noodles in bowl and stir in grated cheese.

Sweet and Sour Ramen Chicken

Serves: 3-4

Ingredients:

2 (3 oz) packages chicken-flavored ramen noodles
1 cup bell pepper, chopped (red or green, your choice)
1/2 teaspoon ginger
4 whole green onions, thinly sliced
1 (20 oz) can pineapple chunks in juice, un-drained
1 lb boneless chicken breasts
oil as needed
1/2 cup sweet and sour sauce

Directions:

1. Drain the pineapple juice into a measuring cup and add enough water to measure 2 cups; set aside.

2. Cut the chicken into 1-inch pieces and season with ginger.

3. Heat a bit of oil and stir fry the chicken for 3-4 minutes.

4. Add the pineapple juice and bring to a boil.

5. Break the noodles into pieces and add to the skillet with the seasoning packets.

6. Bring back to a boil, reduce the heat, and simmer for 3 minutes until the noodles are tender and most of the liquid is absorbed.

7. Add the sweet and sour sauce, pepper, onion, and pineapple.

8. Cook until the peppers are tender.

Taco Ramen Bowls

Serves: 2

Ingredients:

1 (3 oz) package any flavor ramen noodles
1/2 lb lean hamburger
2 Tbsp finely chopped onions
3/4 cup can diced tomato, drained
2 Tbsp taco seasoning
1 cup water
1/4 cup shredded Mexican blend cheese
1/4 cup crushed tortilla chips
sour cream (garnish)
salsa (garnish)

Directions:

1. Brown meat with onion and drain.

2. Stir in tomatoes, taco seasoning and water. Bring to a boil.

3. Add ramen noodles and save the seasoning package for another recipe.

4. Cook and stir for 3 to 5 minutes or until noodles are tender.

5. Spoon into bowls and sprinkle with cheese and tortilla chips.

6. Serve with sour cream and salsa for additional garnish.

Tomato Ramen Soup

Serves: 1-2

Ingredients:

1 (3 oz) package any flavor ramen noodles
2 cups water
1 can tomato soup

Directions:

1. Cook noodles as directed on package. Do not drain.

2. Add tomato soup concentrate.

3. Simmer five minutes.

Uncommon Ramen BBQ Chicken Pizza Bake

Serves: 2-4

Ingredients:

2 (3 oz) packages any flavor ramen noodles
1/2 cup milk
1 egg, beaten
1/4 cup parmesan cheese, grated
1 cup barbecue sauce (use your favorite)
1 cup cooked chicken, chopped
1/2 red onion, sliced thinly (preferably sweet onion)
11 oz mandarin oranges, drained well
2 cups mozzarella cheese, grated
black olives (optional)
mushroom (optional)
canned jalapeno slices (optional)
bell pepper (optional)
red pepper flakes (optional)

Directions:

1. Bring water to a boil and cook ramen noodles. Save the seasoning packets for another recipe.

2. Meanwhile, beat egg and whisk together with milk and parmesan cheese.

3. Drain noodles well and add to egg mixture.

4. Line a pizza pan with aluminum foil and spray with non-stick cooking spray.

5. Spread noodle mixture evenly onto pan.

6. Spread barbecue sauce over noodles and scatter chicken, onions, and oranges on top.

Uncommon Ramen BBQ Chicken Pizza Bake, cont.

7.   Spread mozzarella cheese evenly over all.

8.   Bake at 350° for 20 minutes or until brown.

9.   Let stand 5 minutes before slicing.

Veggie Ramen

Serves: 1

Directions:

1 (3 oz) package any flavor ramen noodles
2 cups water
1 cup mixed veggies (fresh, frozen or canned)

Ingredients:

1. Cook noodles according to package directions with the veggies and drain.

2. Add seasoning packet.